Life Finds Its Way

Reflections On Reality With Sabyasachi Guha

~

Nandini Kapadia

Life Finds Its Way

Reflections On Reality With Sabyasachi Guha

Nandini Kapadia

A Division of Maoli Media Private Limited

This book is dedicated to my late father
Trilochan Amritlal Kapadia
with love

Life Finds Its Way
Reflections On Reality With Sabyasachi Guha

First Edition: May 2019

PUBLISHED BY

ZEN PUBLICATIONS

A Division of Maoli Media Private Limited

60, Juhu Supreme Shopping Centre,
Gulmohar Cross Road No. 9, JVPD Scheme,
Juhu, Mumbai 400 049. India.
Tel: +91 9022208074
eMail: info@zenpublications.com
Website: www.zenpublications.com

Published in collaboration with
Parting Shot Press, USA
partingshot1213@gmail.com

Cover & Book Design: Red Sky Designs, Mumbai

Cover Image: © Kishor Chopda
Back Cover Image: © Julie Clark Thayer
Images on page 8, 14: © Kishor Chopda

ISBN 978-93-87242-35-7

Printed By
SAP Print Solutions Pvt. Ltd.

Contents

Sabyasachi Guha

A Biographical Sketch

He is a man whose most common refrain is joyous laughter. He considers the day he met U.G. Krishnamurti as the most important day of his life. Sabyasachi Guha was working as a research scientist in a field of physics called "superconductivity" when he met the elusive Krishnamurti at a friend's apartment in New York City. With a background in hatha yoga and meditation from childhood, Guha was also a serious reader of Jiddu Krishnamurti (JK) and when he came to meet U.G. for the first time, he was ready to be dissuaded from his spiritual pursuits. The words he'd read in U.G.'s books seemed at first to imply such a result. Instead, his contact with U.G. was to change the course of his life in a very different way.

A rebellious lad, Guha was sent off to a boarding school run by his mother's guru in Bengal for two years where he routinely recited the Bhagavad Gita and practiced prayer meditations. Many a time during school breaks, he would put his bicycle on a boat, cross the Ganges and ride to Dakshineshwar temple, home to the famous saint of Bengal, Sri Ramakrishna. There he would meditate in the room where the saint spent most of his days. "Nothing ever happened in that room," he laughed as he told me this anecdote.

After reading a biography of Albert Einstein the young Guha developed a passionate interest in physics and went from being a soccer-crazy youth and a mediocre student to joining the celebrated Presidency College in Calcutta. Never one to take the easy route, within a year he joined an underground revolutionary political party, left his home and his studies and ended up on the run from the law, living as a fugitive in Varanasi. Late one night while sitting on the ghats with his boatmen friends a young corpse floated up underfoot. Faced with the brutal evidence of his own mortality, the question of what his life meant in the scheme of things grabbed his attention with unmistakable intensity.

After a year, his life in hiding came to an end and he turned his attention back to his studies. Guha completed his PhD in physics from the Indian Institute of Science, India's premier research center in Bangalore. During his studies he discovered the teachings of JK on the library shelves. Despite the demands on the time of a student in the highest levels of physics, Guha says, he read every book of JK thoroughly. After earning his degree, he was immediately recruited to work for the prestigious Indian Space Research Organization.

When his wife, herself a highly qualified crystallographer, came to the United States as a post-doctoral fellow, Guha followed and began working as a research scientist in the field of superconductivity at Rutgers University in New Jersey. Living the life of a family man with his wife and two young daughters, he continued his spiritual research as well, taking his family with him on endless meditation retreats in America and abroad as he became more deeply involved with the Ram Chandra Mission. In 1995, Guha discovered the website of U.G. Krishnamurti whose books were freely available online. Surprised by the utter dismissal of spiritual pursuits expressed in U.G.'s books, Guha was shaken to the core by a unique expression he could not explain. The books disturbed him deeply. Despite all the efforts he put in his spiritual practices and the "progress" he was assured he was making by the members of the mission, he was dissatisfied with the results. In this respect, U.G. resonated with him acutely. "His words were throwing me into a state of confusion. Then the thought came to me one day on my way to office, if there was a person like Sri Ramakrishna around, wouldn't I go and see him? I contacted the person from the website again and as it turned out U.G. was due in New York the following day."

As these things sometimes happened with U.G., Guha was invited to see him right away. Arriving first thing in the morning the two spent the entire day deep in discussion. That evening when he returned home he became physically ill. Thinking he must be suffering from a bout of flu or malaria, neither of these explanations made sense. Later, he related these symptoms to U.G. and was surprised at the response, "You see when you come here you are putting yourself into trouble." "I thought U.G. was joking when he said 'you wouldn't touch this with a ten-foot barge poll.' Now I know he was damn serious. There were nights when I thought this was the last night of my life."

Guha poured body and soul into the time he spent with U.G. and U.G. made sure Guha brought his family along whenever he visited. Trusting the powerful example before him, he was able to withstand all kinds of physical reactions and experiences around U.G. that he said he neither understood nor eventually felt the need to justify. U.G. illustrated the functionality of a body free from the stranglehold of thought whose expression could not be separated from that functioning. This may explain why people so often get wrong impressions from reading the books alone, something U.G. warned against. "So many mistakes have been made by people taking these words literally."

Early on, while he was experiencing disturbing physical symptoms, Guha asked about the physical impact of U.G.'s company, putting it to him as a statement more than a question… "U.G., I have asked you and you have told me all these things, (speaking about U.G.'s denials of spiritual matters), and yet something is happening to me." The response was clear, "It is out of your hands. It is out of my hands. Just leave it alone."

By leaving it alone, Guha eventually discovered for himself the implications of what U.G. was hinting at all the time. Speaking from his own point of view, Guha addresses the already existing order the human body is trying to maintain within itself to function at maximum capacity while thought is constantly pulling us, as it were, in the opposite direction. As he put it in one conversation, "There is nothing to defend in this, nothing to justify." Confidence in the body is not something that can be passed along to a listener through verbal understanding. U.G. eventually recognized in his own encounters with people that words lead to nothing more than the usual delusions of grandeur that come from habitual self-aggrandizement in the name of information gathering. I for one, think this explains some of the changes in his mode of expression over different periods of time, yet the fundamental message was unwavering and uncompromising.

Guha has always focused on the need to give space to the life force we are all a part of, as it is expressed in the basic functions of the body. The trust that we can and will survive if we can just leave it alone to function at its own level comes at its own pace. Left to its own devices, it becomes obvious that this body is already taking care of itself without the collection of ideas that makes up a personality, ego, whatever word you want to use. U.G. used to hammer this point home by pointing out the extraordinary efficiency of the system that already sustains us. "This is not my natural state. It is also yours! Do we give permission to the heart to pump blood? Do we need to learn pranayama in order to breathe?"

After many years with U.G. Guha said the worries for the future and his family were obliterated from his system. There was no dramatic 'calamity,' there was no tragic break with his family as happened with U.G. In fact, the story of his life is nothing like the story of U.G.'s.

U.G. would tell Guha in his easily overlooked, joking way, "You are responsible for solving the energy crisis!" Perhaps the crisis we face as a species as well as individuals, can be resolved if we allow ourselves the kind of space Guha is pointing to. This is something that only happens once you stop looking outside for answers. Easier said than done. The system that keeps all of us on this merry-go-round is deeply embedded in the core habits fueled by the basic fear that keeps societal demands in charge within us. Spiritual fantasies of living as a hermit, or putting a stop to the thoughts of society through meditation were dismissed by U.G. as absurd. As Guha puts it, "One has to face the danger of the water hole. Society is that water hole. Through thinking we have the tools to get what we need to survive in this society. Words and thoughts are our tools, talents are also tools which enable us to survive; they are perfectly natural in their place."

– Louis Brawley
Author of *Goner* (USA) and
No More Questions: Final Travels of U.G. Krishnamurti (India)

~

Author's Note

"If you have someone like Guha in your life, your life is made," Luna Tarlo, author and long-time friend of Sabyasachi Guha always said. I could not agree more. There are two reasons for this. Firstly, Guha's total and unconditional acceptance of whomsoever knocks on his door. No questions asked, no impositions made and one true friend to call your own. Secondly, over time, you will be astonished to discover that you are interacting with an extraordinary human being who while living in society is completely detached from its push and pull. To use a scriptural metaphor, Guha is like a swan swimming in water but is totally uncontaminated by it. Such a presence or energy is bound to affect you in some manner or another depending on how closely you are aligned with it. Then you are "hooked" for good.

I am fortunate that I could spend long hours with Guha in intense discussions day in day out and also accompany him around the globe. It gave me the rare opportunity to witness at close hand how this enigma called Guha led his life, dealt with people and the effect he had on them, including me, of course. The more I tried to fathom him the more I was confounded because I could never "find" Guha. All I saw in him was my own reflection, my conditioning at play. After months of witnessing the goings-on around him, the drive to document these unique phenomena came with full force and the seed for this book was sown.

Life Finds Its Way is my debut offering which documents

one-and-a-half-years (2015-2016) of my close association with Guha. Like a mother tending to a newborn, I have nurtured my story with infinite tenderness and care. Allowing my inner voice to guide me, I was startled to see what kept emerging from the depths of my being. I realized many of the long-forgotten incidents and events, in retrospect, were instrumental in shaping my life journey. Consequently, what began as a chronicle about life in the time of Guha soon turned into a semi-autobiographical work with characteristic reflectiveness of an embattled seeker.

Dear reader, I urge you to hang on to what Guha is conveying through numerous interactions, especially on the nature of reality because that's where the essence of our existence lays. His quotes, many a time gleaned from lengthy passages, are sprinkled liberally as well as captured in bullet points throughout the book.

Lastly, I take this opportunity to thank my son Agastya and friends Julie, Kamal, Kishor, Radhika, Tanusri and Revathi for their valuable input and help. As for Guha, my muse, no words are forthcoming to express my immense gratitude for his unswerving support.

– Nandini Kapadia
New Jersey, USA
January 27, 2019

~

Introduction

I had the privilege of knowing U.G. Krishnamurti, the most subversive human being ever who shot down the very idea of individual existence as an independent entity entrenched in the colloidal mix called society. Conforming to live in society means living in fear and extending that fear by propagating its norms, foundation of which is born of human thought.

Whenever I was in the proximity of U.G., the feeling of being choked by the pressure came to the fore and a sense of seeking freedom from this stranglehold was felt deep down in my gut. I wondered if there was anyone who was able to benefit from his proximity by way of breaking this barrier which is so deeply hardwired. During the course of my long association with and multiple visits to U.G., I noticed that, at times, there was a jovial gentleman called Guha sitting by his side. He happened to be not just thoroughly enjoying U.G.'s presence but remained a silent and a laughing spectator to the drama unfolding day after day around U.G. as people came to see him and display their wealth of information in matters esoteric. He was so immersed in the energy field of U.G. that nothing mattered to him other than U.G.'s closeness and his words. There was a definite attraction and a seemingly unquestioning submission. After U.G. passed away, I had an urge to meet Guha in the U.S. and soon realized that he had indeed disentangled himself from this stranglehold. It is this freedom that has become the attraction and I can unequivocally state that anyone seeking freedom from the depth of one's being would also be attracted.

One such seeker is the author of this journal, which has now seen the light of day as a full-fledged book, *Life Finds Its Way*. In the first couple of meetings itself, I noticed that Nandini was addressing this same stranglehold of which she is a captive and is ever ready to admit her vulnerability. In Guha, like most of us, she saw no agenda, imposition, abstraction, exploitation or manipulation, all of which are so rampant in the thriving holy business. Upon entering the real world of hard-core spirituality, those seeking equilibrium-imbuing qualities must look at life with utmost honesty, uncolored by the glares of conditioning. It is then that one sees the simplicity and purity of life.

It is due to our conditioning, born out of archaic traditions and patterns of thought entrenched in a "non-living" and invalid culture that we do not recognize this sordidness. It was to expose this stultifying culture and give an uncorrupted view of life that propelled Nandini to document much of what she was hearing straight from the horse's mouth. Her literary background and surprising new association preceded by some heavy doses of bitter experiences in the social context have led her to write about herself and preserve for posterity the golden words and intimate discussions with her mentor and brother-like figure, Guha. In turn, it is endearing to see Guha reflect her sentiments and refer to her as his "sissy".

Thus, was the genesis of *Life Finds Its Way*. I hope you enjoy reading it as much as I did.

– Kamal Grover
Mumbai

~

Chapter One

Boat Against the Current

The idea of fulfillment is not harmony. The idea of loving another and being loved by another is not harmony. What is harmony? When you accept your capacity and know what you can or can't get out of that capacity in the context of the social structure that you're living in, then there is no conflict and you are in harmony.
– Guha

Feb. 26, 2015
Cochin, Kerala

I wake up at 5 am to get an early start to my first day in Cochin with Guha. I join him in the living room and we sit in silence, he with eyes closed and I lost in my own world. I am cherishing these quiet but intense moments because ever since I met Guha I am hooked and want to spend all my time with him. To be honest, earlier I was like a frog in the well or a bird in a cage but with infinite care Guha drew me out and made me leap into the wild, nay, gave me wings to fly to the moon. It's turning out to be a momentous journey.

Outside the sun is slowly rising over the still backwaters spreading a golden glow over the room. I can hear Julie Clark Thayer, my other roomie, puttering around in the kitchen; soon she emerges with coffee and crackers for all of us. The illustrious septuagenarian needs no introduction to those familiar with the name of late U.G. Krishnamurti, iconoclast "non-guru", as she was a prominent star in the U.G. galaxy. All three of us are visiting Cochin, dubbed as the Queen of the Arabian Sea, for the first time. I am upbeat and full of excitement as this is also the first time I will be staying here with the eminent duo for a couple of weeks and later accompany them across India to meet friends. Guha looks fresh as the morning dew although none of us slept a wink last night. I could hear his phone go ding, ding and tring tring all night. Good friends Revathi and Radhika (popularly known as R & R) from Yankland desperately trying to connect with him, I surmised.

The sound of the doorbell ringing interrupts my reverie and I see Manoj entering with a hot beverage in his hand. Manoj is our next door neighbor and a recent addition to the Guha family. It was at his invitation that Guha and friends are here. Sanjiv and Kishor are next to arrive. Hailing from Mumbai, they are being accommodated by Manoj for their entire stay. All of us are raring to ask Guha some serious fundamental questions. Guha feels the energy and starts off with:

- *Utopia does not exist.*
- *There's nobody running the show.*
- *How do I solve the problem? Waiting for an answer is not going to work. There is no how. Nature never asks such questions.*
- *You can never, never capture it.*
- *I don't have a mission. Mission means what? You think you have found something which will save, enrich humanity.*
- *To my utter dismay I found that there is nothing there that is representative of me.*
- *The authority that came out of the social context is the wrong authority.*

- *The sense of self, the 'I' which is seeking relief, IS the cause of all problems.*
- *We are all unique but not special.*

We listen with rapt attention as Guha begins to elaborate on his pet topic – "subject specific functional reality". He says it was his general observation that the way one individual's brain creates reality for himself can never be the exact same as anyone else's. "What is obvious for me is so damn difficult to convince others. Why is it so? Why is it that someone's absolute certainty about a particular thing is impossible for me to accept? For example, you may look at the sky and see something but when I look at the sky I don't see anything. These are the type of questions that came out of my own observations." Thus, Guha emphasizes, each and every person on the planet is unique and since everybody's system is differently organized we tend to look at life through our own distinct "filter". The same mechanism also governs our reaction or response to any given situation. This, he terms, is our subjective functional reality and that is all there is. Guha categorically denies the concept of reality as described in the scriptures and declares, "There is no such thing as ultimate or absolute reality."

While discussions are raging on the nature of reality, Julie is in la la land. The minute Guha starts talking, she invariably goes into "yoga nidra". I have been observing this phenomenon day in day out ever since I first met both of them, but it never fails to amaze me. After U.G.'s death in 2007, Julie has been a close friend and a travel companion to Guha. When I asked her how she became so close knit with Guha and his family she replied, "I think it was U.G. who set it up this way; I see his hand in this."

For Julie it was love at first sight the day she met U.G. in California in the spring of 1989. He must have had a tremendous effect on her because she dumped her "guru" Andrew Cohen and returned home. In Preface to her personal diary *Travels with U.G. Krishnamurti,* she recounts, "I . . . . made the acquaintance of a man who was to play the most remarkable role in my life from that moment on." A couple of months later, she called U.G. and invited him to use her apartment in New York, an offer he surprisingly accepted. He arrived at her doorstep on a damp September day holding a small suitcase and declared he had come to stay for "forty days and forty nights". That day happened to be Julie's 49th birthday. This was the end of life as Julie knew it and the beginning of the U.G. epoch. She admits, "I began keeping a journal from the first day. Somehow, I felt his visit was going to be interesting, epic . . . ."

In her book, Julie gives an up, close and a very personal account of her first two years with U.G. Her trials and tribulations while trying to align with U.G. and the mind shattering impact his proximity had on her immediately strike a chord with the reader. She continued to travel extensively with him for more than two decades although there were times when she was utterly tormented by the onslaught of mental movements brought about by his powerful presence. Perhaps she sensed what was coming because in the Preface she confesses, "...yet a power emanated from him that turned my brain to slush". Her struggles remind me of what the wise men of yore warned thousands of years ago: *The path to salvation is narrow and as difficult to walk as a razor's edge.*

The human mind has a tendency to compare and contrast and I am tempted to juxtapose Julie's relationship to U.G., the "roaring sage", alongside that of Suri Nagamma's to Ramana Maharshi, the sage of Arunachala. Even though the time, place and context differ vastly, their "love stories" captivate me. Suri Nagamma, like Julie, adored her guru from the very first time she met him. Born in 1902 in a small village in south India, Nagamma had a tragic life. She lost both her parents before she was ten. At the age of eleven, she got married but within a year was widowed. For many years she was in a state of shock but gradually she taught herself to read and write. As years went by, she immersed herself in scriptures and had a longing to meet a real guru.

Eventually, Nagamma came on a pilgrimage to Ramanasram in Tiruvannamalai in 1941 and never left; she was completely enamored by Ramana. In those days, women were not allowed to live in the ashram so she chose to live on her own close to Ramana's abode. From 1945 onwards, she started writing letters in her native Telugu to her brother who was living elsewhere, describing to him day to day life in the ashram and her interactions with Ramana, her deity. The epistles were then compiled in the famed book *Letters from Sri Ramanasramam* and later translated into English. Nagamma had surrendered her life to Ramana who in turn was very kind and affectionate towards her, like a father to a daughter. For Julie, it was more like playing with fire, trying not to get engulfed in the towering inferno at the same time. Ultimately, they both found salvation by way of immense love and devotion to their gurus.

Guha is still talking but I'm not paying much attention, just feel happy to be here. We are in a place called Maradu, about thirty kilometers from Cochin airport where Manoj, his wife Vidya and their nine-year-old son live. Our apartment located on the thirteenth floor is numbered 13G. In Hindi it would translate to "tera G" meaning "your G". How apt since it is occupied by our G! The flat is big, airy, nicely furnished, and has a huge, fully-equipped kitchen. The living room has a long balcony and offers an endless vista of tranquil waters and lush greenery. I step out for stunning views of water, water everywhere, as far as the eyes can see. A few fishermen are rowing their little round boats while I am intrigued by the giant Chinese fishing net erected on the water's edge which looks more like a contraption to catch a whale! How pretty it all looks, just like a picture-perfect postcard.

Feb. 27, 2015

Last night too I could not get much sleep although I had a hectic day and was exhausted. Plus, the room was very hot and humid despite the overhead fan whirring at top speed all night. I am feeling despondent since I have not spoken to K since I arrived here. I hear him talking to Guha several times a day but for some reason he has not called me. In the morning, bleary eyed and a little cranky, I could not resist asking Guha: "If I am having physical discomfort like feeling very hot or very cold, is it due to conditioning?" Guha's reply, "The best way to resolve the issue is to eliminate all mental movements that produce highs or lows; what remains is the result of reality. Then you can find a proper remedy." Take that, I mutter to myself.

After a quick shower, I am ready for whatever the day brings. First, I greet Bubu, short for Subhashish who arrived from Kolkata last evening. He is an old friend of Guha and a singer by profession who travels frequently to give performances all over India and abroad. Since Guha forbade Bubu to divulge his (Guha's) whereabouts to anyone in Kolkata, he told his wife that he was flying to Cochin on a professional assignment. Guha does not want a certain someone to get the whiff of his arrival here. The lady in question is a frequent visitor to Kolkata and is in close contact with Guha's friends there.

I smile looking at the motley crowd. Manoj is a diehard U.G. follower who never met U.G. All his time was devoted reading U.G. books, listening to audio talks and watching U.G. videos on YouTube. The intensity with which he did this was such that he can talk for hours like U.G., even emulating his hero with authentic gestures and mannerisms! Manoj had been reading Guha's talks online but met him for the first time in Kolkata only a few months ago. One meeting was enough to make him cancel his other plans and travel with Guha instead. He and his family relocated to Cochin recently. An IT professional he is currently working for his US-based brother's start-up. Sanjiv, the quiet one, too was a U.G. fan. He lives in Mumbai and is proprietor of an interior decorating firm. Both Manoj and Sanjiv stumbled upon Guha's website while looking for U.G. material online. Kishor, whose theatric repartees keep us amused, is self-employed but is almost retired. He has always been spiritually inclined and was in close association with Ranjit Maharaj, brother disciple of Nisargadatta Maharaj. Incidentally, Ranjit Maharaj passed away just a year after Kishor first met him. Kishor and Sanjiv are good friends and live close by. Kishor had not even heard of Guha until Sanjiv introduced them in Mumbai the day before we were to leave for Cochin. Then, on the spur of the moment he decided to join us. That's how we are all gathered here.

We want to explore the neighborhood and get some exercise, so we all put on our walking shoes and head out. Soon we are traversing the narrow lanes of the small village nearby which is lined with modest cottages on both sides. There is hardly any space for such a large group to walk together but we file past quickly cracking jokes while local folks, young and old, give us curious looks. Despite looking unpretentious and unassuming, I am certain they are well educated as Kerala has the highest literacy rate in India. Nursing is a top profession for the women who have found lucrative careers in Gulf countries. The hamlet is soon left behind as we continue to trudge along the dirt road towards the waterside. This expanse is covered with abundant coconut, palm and mango trees, thick banana groves and even some drumsticks trees. There is not a cloud in the sky and the sun is shining bright hot by now. With cool waters beckoning we quicken our pace and soon reach the muddy bank. Far from the madding crowd I take a deep breath in the fresh, invigorating air. A fisherman in umbrella hat rowing afar, crows cawing, a dog barking, gentle ripples appearing and disappearing endlessly in the water – in Guha's presence the mundane seems magical.

The first thing, as usual, we have a photo session in our new surroundings. Julie loves to click as photography is her lifelong passion having published volumes of her work. In fact, she has a fantastic photo collection of U.G. and Guha. We stand around forming a half circle trading light banter. Plenty of laughter and joviality in Guha's energy field, that's his trademark. Afterwards Guha looks at me smilingly and offers to take me rowing in a canoe. He knows I am afraid of water and cannot swim. I jocularly reply, "Why don't you walk over the water, like Jesus did? I can walk with you." Guha retorts, "I can take you across the river by this boat, I don't need to walk on the water. As for Jesus walking on water, U.G. would say it was fortunate for Jesus that the water was only knee-deep and unfortunate for humanity." I decline the offer saying I would not enjoy the ride. Pat came the reply, "Pathways of life are not full of roses!"

It is mid-morning and we have just returned home from our invigorating walk. The word "home" comes naturally to my mind because Guha and Julie are like my family and living under the same roof with them feels like home, sweet home. Secretly, I think of Guha as my elder brother whose only concern is my core well-being. After breakfast we head next door. Another round of tea/coffee over, Guha and Manoj are engaged in serious talks, Julie is sound asleep, Bubu is taking videos and photos, including some selfies, and Sanjiv and Kishor are eagerly waiting for Guha to continue from where he left off earlier. Guha is ready:

- *The primary sound is the mother's words. These words are the most powerful. Your habitual response to that sound gives you the feeling that there's someone inside. They give you an apparent center. That's not in the space of life. It is imaginary.*
- *Belief structure: How the belief forms from the fantastic perceptive capacity of this organism. If you don't do that you are dead.*
- *The image-making faculty called the will is the problem maker, not the problem solver. You say I accept that I have a festering wound inside me that has to be taken care of now. But that acceptance of yours has no punch. You still have hope. You can't even accept something small like unknowability (of the way life moves).*
- *The system knows this thought will not serve any useful purpose, so it will not allow it to have any impact on the system.*

- *When you pose the most difficult challenge to your brain it becomes obsessed with finding a solution and brings out its own unique resolution.*
- *When the competition for mere survival is so fierce, so hard to get, the intention which has an imaginative faculty, gives life to what is illusory.*
- *Nobody has any power unless you give power to them.*
- *The world is going to run out of resources very soon. Every single tree will be your furniture.*
- *I'll sing my song and go. I'm ready now.*

The value system gets Guha all riled up. He decries, "You want to be a Buddha, you want to find the state of Ramana! You are always trying to exemplify somebody, appreciate somebody and in the process never value yourself. You are already in every sense of the term functioning the way you are supposed to be functioning. Your wanting something to be other than what you are is one of the most important reasons for your unhappiness, misery, sorrow, etc. You can't accept who you are. Somebody told you that you are bad, and you accepted that. Somebody told you that you are an idiot and you accepted that. Somebody tells you that you are ugly, and you accept that, then go inside your bedroom and cry for three days. All your life you will make efforts to look better. It's a beautiful life and you are wasting it."

Guha's statement *you can't accept who you are* sends shivers down my spine. It takes me back to my teens when I willy nilly joined a cultish group called The Path, later renamed Lifewave. The self-proclaimed head of this organization was an Irishman named John Yarr from the UK, who formerly belonged to the Divine Life Mission. John thought he was "enlightened" and called himself Ishvara. In fact, he had even spread rumors that he had done rigorous *tapasya* and stood on one leg for three days and three nights before he got liberation. The main ideology of the Path was to find enlightenment by ascending to higher planes of consciousness through initiation into divine light and divine sound. And John was the new avatara, the new Buddha, the perfect master who was qualified to open that gateway for deserving aspirants. In retrospect, the whole thing was a mishmash of Theosophical, Advaita Vedanta, Shabd Yoga and Shaktipat doctrines. An amusing aside: John who was supposedly a big fan of J Krishnamurti, sent someone to JK to inform him that the new Buddha (John) had arrived. Not surprisingly, JK got angry and threw him out.

As with most cult leaders, Johnny's modus operandi was to control his brood through fear and mind control. Although no one said it openly, we were fearful of displeasing him, fearful of displeasing the group leader and fearful of stepping out of line. Asking too many questions or raising doubts was out too because that would automatically amount to insubordination and lack of faith, putting you back at the end of the queue for initiation. Another technique he used was to alienate us from family and friends unless they were also his followers. We were brainwashed to such a degree that we kept ourselves aloof from near and dear ones. One of my fellow practitioners who was a medical student at the time was so indoctrinated that she would whisper in every newborn's ear, 'Ishvara is here'. Another one stopped calling his parents mom, dad and addressed them by their first names, which is unheard of in our culture. As if this overbearing, stifling atmosphere where the most basic human freedoms were snatched away was not enough, we also had to follow strict injunctions. Regular attendance at local discourses, doing service at Lifewave centers, adopting a vegetarian diet and so on were a must otherwise you would be disqualified. Sexual intercourse was only permitted between married couples although Johnny was allegedly a pedophile and had a history of sexual misconduct. In fact, that was what led to his downfall and the organization was disbanded in 1986.

One may ask why I got attracted to such a clique. I can put

forth any number of reasons but the bottom line is sub-consciously I was punishing myself for my conceived short comings and imperfections. I was a tormented teen, to use a cliché, always finding fault with myself – I was not beautiful enough, talented enough or smart enough. I constantly berated myself for my "failings" and never acknowledged my own strengths or value myself for what I am. The value system, the role models created by society made it impossible for me to blossom into my own, all the while doubting my innate abilities and talents. In short, I could not accept myself the way I was and was looking for a way out. Perhaps Lifewave would redeem me. Moreover, my brother Dev was one of the founding members of this group in Mumbai and I looked up to him for everything. His approval was important to me. Subtly, it was made clear to me that until I followed the Path I was wasting my life away. My best friend was also sucked into Lifewave creating a big void in my life then. I held back as long as I could but ultimately gave in. Fortunately, just a few months after my "initiation", the whole thing went kaput.

Suddenly, Guha's oft-repeated pronouncement *I am a dropout from the game of social dynamics* flashes in my mind. When I urge him to elaborate he replies, "I do not pursue ways and means to seek approval or justification from the social structure. All endeavors of the human intellect are a game of social dynamics. One day I decided to stop playing the game. It has no meaning to me, but I continue doing it because there is no way out. I have no role models. No godman, religious or scientific authority can create a value system in me. Those who created the value system are totally insignificant."

Back to my musings, I met my future husband (now ex) in Lifewave who was even more of a lost soul than I was. Although bright and talented, he was completely burnt out, so to speak, and his friends had given him a fitting nickname of "old man". A chemical engineer from an elite university, he barely managed to get his degree after ten years. He was a hardcore drug addict and a heavy drinker before he turned over a new leaf while pursuing meditation. Perhaps

Lifewave gave him the hope of redemption but when it broke up all his old problems resurfaced. He was already in his thirties when I married him, but he had no job, no money, no house and a host of mental, psychological issues, the last I realized when it was way too late. The love and affection, the stability that I craved he could not deliver and how much ever I tried to get our relationship on track, only backfired. The marriage was a total disaster from the onset and after seventeen agonizing years he walked out one day. Now again, one may ask why did I marry such a man? My excuse is I was a victim of circumstance. I could not stay at home and I could not pull out. Given my own emotional complexes I thought at least he loved me, we could work things out. How naïve I was.

My home life was far from serene. Since I was a little girl I have been hypersensitive to my immediate surroundings and pick up vibes around me very quickly. Unfortunately, my childhood environment was highly toxic which left an indelible scar on my psychological make-up. It destroyed my self-confidence and I was under perpetual stress, seething with anger and discontent. Unwittingly, I fell into a destructive pattern of rebellion, guilt, self-pity, self-doubt and self-denial, leading to chronic headaches and anorexia. Perhaps that was instrumental in making wrong life choices. Who knows? So, I beat on, a small boat against the social current, borne back ceaselessly into the past, unable to move forward in life till I saw Guha waving the green light.[1]

~

1 *Adapted from F. Scott Fitzgerald's* The Great Gatsby

Chapter Two

Energy of Change

Once the natural order is established in the system it forces the system's character into a different operational mode. All interaction is on demand and once the work is over the demand is gone; the system meditates into itself and rejuvenates to gain the supreme vitality by being alone. The scriptures call that state 'kaivalya'.

– Guha

Feb. 28, 2015

It is not yet dawn but we are ready and waiting for Guha. The minute he walks into the room Manoj sets the ball rolling for a dynamic discussion. Guha is all pumped up too:

- *If life has a purpose it is always fulfilling it. What you want to know is if that is fulfilling the status quo.*
- *Freedom is to let the system do its job optimally. Then you begin to sense unburdening and peace.*
- *On this planet, those who suffer the most are the ones who have deep beliefs.*
- *When you are truly concerned about another, THERE IS NO YOU.*
- *If you take medications, it increases the frequency of the symptoms.*

- *For you giving up means you are waiting for some positive results. It's a "sauda" or a bargain. That's not giving up.*
- *To overcome the challenges that you are facing, the problems you have, the energy of life has no value. To help you with your struggles you only need one thing – MONEY.*
- *All thinking is "sapna". Thinking is future. That has to go.*
- *The system is not interested in the acceptance of a belief structure. It is a burden.*
- *Your anxiety is based on the knowledge you have about yourself and the future you create or project for yourself. The moment this perceptive universe is replaced with the thought universe, it is all speculation. However, there is some connection. The images of the perceptive universe have some meaning for us and then we recreate images through memory. It is connected to the essence of life that is unfolding in every individual.*
- *Real meditation is when you are not interfering in the way your system is producing a solution to your problem.*

In his talks, Guha often uses the term "system" and I want some clarifications:

I: What exactly do you mean when you refer to the "system"?

Guha: Mind-body.

I: The system is mind-body unit as a whole?

Guha: When I say body, it means the entire physical body and the brain is a part of it; some emergent property of the brain is called consciousness. Human mind is related to self-consciousness.

I: The terms body and system are synonymous?

Guha: Yes.

Suddenly, I feel drained of energy and zone out. Unable to sleep for the third consecutive night, I had woken up this morning again with a throbbing headache. What is it that's keeping me sleepless in Cochin? Can't figure out whether it's the jetlag, job worries or just feeling let down by K. I have been without a job for months, putting me under a lot of pressure over finances. Plus, family issues which have been plaguing me for years tend to get overwhelming at times. Guha wasn't joking when he told me, "There's so much junk inside you," adding quickly, "But you will never let go because if the junk goes, you go and you don't want that!" On another occasion he warned, "You really want two things and that is creating all the pain and stress."

Post lunch, as others take a nap next door, I settle into a quiet corner, my retreat. The periodic solitude allows for deep reflection and helps the system regain its poise. Today I am cogitating on the curious phenomena going on around Guha and the power of his presence on our lives. Here's something to ponder: Have you ever felt as if someone was watching over you? That a guardian angel was covering your back through thick and thin? That's how Guha makes me feel, snug and safe, as if ensconced in a protective cocoon spun by his unconditional love and support. But wait. There's more. I have said it earlier but I will shout from the rooftops again – he injected zing, spice and adventure into my life, hitherto conspicuous by their absence. The 'before' Guha life was like a barren land filled with thorns of strife and loneliness while the 'after' one is looking like a lush green, happy, promised land. They say hankering after happiness is like chasing a butterfly but with the advent of the Guha era, it came chasing me. Here's my version of Nathaniel Hawthorne's butterfly quote:

Happiness is a butterfly
You chase it, you lose it
Sit quietly, peacefully
A miracle you may see
As the winged friend
Comes fluttering by
To alight on your knee

If you have been around Guha, you will palpably feel a tremendous surge of goodwill ever flowing from him which in turn unleashes a beneficial energy of change (EC) and all who are aligned with it experience this, sooner or later. That is Guha's most defining quality. Admittedly, that energy can seem to go both ways - create magic for some, like me, or wreak havoc for others. Whether it is coping with obsessive feelings towards Guha, experiencing peak in creativity or undergoing life changes, it is important to remember that such upheavals are ultimately life-abiding and lead to our core well-being.

Let's start with Radhika, whose all-consuming feelings towards Guha is bound to defy one's wildest logic but there she is, head over heels in love with her G. Married for almost 30 years, she is smart, talented, and a successful career woman. But after being with Guha for some months, she fell madly, deeply in love with him even as other interests began to fade away. Now onwards her life revolved only around Guha with her mind constantly dwelling on him like a tanpura drone going tui, tui, tui (*tu hi* in Hindi means only you) in the background. Whether at work, home, shopping or with friends and family, she would bombard Guha with a million texts a day, unable to bear his absence. Often, she devised to work from Julie's house with the expectation that he would stop by for lunch or coffee. At other times, if Guha was busy at home, she would wait patiently for hours, either in a park, a mall or languish in her car nearby in case he took mercy on her and invite her inside. Once she played hooky from work and got on the bus to the city where he was staying even though he explicitly forbade her to visit him. On another occasion, while hosting a party, she surreptitiously slipped away from home to drop off a bowl of soup she had prepared specially for her beloved. She had to leave it at Julie's house because Guha barred her from visiting him as he was busy with guests from India. Guha has scolded her many times not to indulge in such tactics, but Radhika remains undeterred. Her single-minded devotion to her guiding light and liberator has been causing problems with her family too, but she refuses to compromise. Watching her sitting next to him, sometimes with eyes closed, sometimes with tears oozing out of her eyelids, it is safe to conclude that Guha is her sole life support and without him her life would be insufferable.

To win over Guha was no mean feat for Radhika, there being times when she almost gave up in despair. After the initial "honeymoon" period, Guha came down hard on her, occasionally even voicing his anger and disapproval with strong words. Perhaps he was testing her, who knows, but the indefatigable Radhika weathered every Guha storm that came her way with infinite resilience. Fortunately, her love story has a happy ending with the wheel of fortune turning in her favor. Inferring from her beaming smiles and happy, chirpy demeanor, Guha is "captured" in the web of love and care she has woven around him. No doubt Guha caters to everyone's needs but nowadays he is indeed quite tender and attentive towards her. This modern-day Mira Bai's[2] full-frontal expression of love towards her Krishna is a timely reminder of what U.G. once pointed out to Guha, "Love is the only way."

Then there's Gina* who has been with Guha since U.G.'s death and her possessiveness towards him can get out of bounds occasionally. Recently, a minor fracas took place when she literally came to blows with another longtime companion of Guha, Angela*, whom she might have been envious of and perceived as a threat. In the heat of the moment, Gina roughly shoved Angela out of the main door of the flat the latter was sharing with Guha in India. Unable to control Gina and before things got out of control, Guha called the police to intervene. Thankfully, no one was badly hurt. We all have shades of jealousy in us and that energy can be suffocating and difficult to cope with at times, resulting in such bizarre episodes. I have seen things get amplified in a heartbeat around Guha where even the most pragmatic find they are riding an emotional roller coaster.

---

2. Mira Bai was a 12th century saint who was devoted to Krishna.

** Names changed*

A few months after I met Guha, a reboot or realignment in the system seemed to take place as mental blocks began to crumble one by one and for the first time I could sense the right balance to function optimally. Next, two main events occurred back to back which catapulted me into a thrilling new phase in my life. First, he introduced me to one of his closest friends K, who swept me off my feet with his kindness, support and earthy, rock solid friendship, more so because it had the element of surprise in it. Who would have thought that besides Guha I would have another close ally, a partner by my side? I was happy as a lark! Secondly, I was fired from my job which was hanging like a noose around my neck anyway. Guha would laugh looking at my downcast expression on a Sunday evening, as if I was going to be hanged on doomsday Monday. Good riddance or as Guha so succinctly quoted from Patanjali's *Yoga Sutras, 'klesa karma nivritti ...'*

On a lighter note, whenever Guha introduced me to someone, with eyes twinkling, he would add the qualifier that I was in the "jobless state". The great storyteller that he is, he would then proceed with glee to describe how I was fired and the battle royal I had to fight in court with my eccentric ex-employer to receive unemployment income. The cunning fox of a boss tried to prove that I was ineligible for my rightful welfare benefits by falsely claiming I was self-employed. But the wacky weirdo was the cause of his own undoing. In front of the judge, the bloke foolishly brandished a worksheet meticulously detailing the number of trespasses I had made to Guha's website while I was working there. The poor judge was scratching her head trying to figure out how this irrelevant information proved that I was self-employed. By this time, Guha's audience is usually doubled up with laughter waiting with bated breath to hear the grand finale. And Guha does not disappoint as with a great flourish he declares, "The dunderhead didn't stand a chance; he lost the case!" As we have all learnt, taking up cudgels against Guha is a thankless task.

The ensuing months were exhilarating as I got to spend vast chunks of time with Guha. Together all three of us, Guha, Julie and I, were busy working round the clock on his forthcoming book. I was honored that he trusted my editing skills and let me be a part of this all-important project. On account of being in Guha's company for long hours, listening to lively discussions as well as witnessing his deft dealings with people, I was beginning to find my own voice, rebuilding my self-confidence and developing a whole new perspective on life. Around Guha everything appeared novel, exciting and always with a sense that anything was possible. Moreover, his healing presence not only acted like a balm but infused my brain, bogged down by years of dross, with new energy and vigor.

Next, Guha continually encouraged me to write and slowly ignited my zeal to put pen to paper. I was a voracious reader from early age but never took up writing except to submit an odd news article or an essay. Once while in eighth grade I recall hiding in a corner and devouring *Gone With the Wind* the day I was to appear for my math exam. Needless to say, I barely passed math but went on to get a master's degree in Literature followed by a career in editing.

When we were in Kolkata, I bought a small notebook and placed it in his hands, pleading him to inaugurate it. Here's what Guha wrote – *You Say the Way You See.* Ever since, I am striving to act upon this seemingly simple advice. I am confident that the EC, the propitious energy I talked about earlier, will be my guiding light and help me create something deeply meaningful and satisfying to me. As I get going, I am shocked to see all that we have learned to face in life is present in our creations and not one thing is forgotten.

Meanwhile, my other newfound friendship, which had taken off so spectacularly, was cruising along smoothly on cloud nine. The rapport between us was growing by leaps and bounds with each passing day. We talked for hours together and marveled at the similarity in our values, goals and aspirations while never losing sight of the fact that our ties were secured under Guha's watch, which felt quite reassuring.

We vowed to keep our bond fresh like a lily in a pond and not allow it to be contaminated by ennui. For such once-in-a-lifetime connection I am indebted to Guha forever. I could not ask for more.

Oh, and one more interesting thing happened – I was bitten by the bug of wanderlust. I wanted to spread my wings and fly far, far away and explore the world like the migratory seabird of the Arctic which travels thousands of miles each year. I wanted to be like Guha, Julie and others who are all free spirits, ready to take off at a moment's notice. But first things first. My fear of driving long distance faded as I began to do sixty miles back and forth to meet Guha. Hitherto, I never went too far on my own. With Guha by my side, for the first time ever I managed to drive hundred and thirty miles to Baltimore to drop off my son Agastya to college. Incidentally, Guha graciously presented him a beautiful pen and an Illy coffee machine as farewell gifts. I later learnt that Agastya had earned fame on campus giving lessons on making outstanding Illy Espressos.

I tagged along with Guha on day trips to New York where many people come to meet him regularly. Julie has a studio apartment in midtown which they call the "office". Alongside intense talks and passionate deliberations, I was exploring the mighty queen of cities like never before. With Guha and Julie as my escorts, we would meander through Central Park admiring the antics of street performers, have coffee and cakes in pricey cafes, shop for olives and mozzarella in Fairway supermarket or stop at Kayser, Julie's favorite German bakery, to pick up freshly baked bread and muffins. Priceless!

It was really exciting to reacquaint myself with the throbbing, pulsating energy of this amazing metropolis, a modern-day cultural Mecca. Passing by Fifth Avenue gawking at swanky shops, enjoying the spirited acrobatics of street performers, smirking at hawkers selling fake Rolexes and Coach bags, watching children slurping on Italian ices and beggars with hats rummaging through trash cans, I was thoroughly immersed in the New York state of mind. Let's not forget to mention the glitzy, glamorous Times Square, a world destination. One of the busiest tourist areas on the planet teeming with throngs of masses all year round, the razzle dazzle created here is a feast for the eyes with glittering, towering billboards, eye-catching Broadway marquees and flashing neon lights. Unforgettable!

The routine continued for some months until one Fall day Guha announced we would be flying to Kolkata to meet his buddies. I was, of course, thrilled at the prospect of traveling with him. Although I had been to the City of Joy many years ago, this time it all looked different as I was seeing it through Guha's eyes. I was also able to experience firsthand the intensity with which he gave of himself for long hours.

Here's a glimpse of our daily routine: Guha's doors would open at 5 am and all would eagerly join him for the first coffee of the day. This was a time of silence for the most part. If someone asked a question, they were likely to get a sharp, terse reply. I am ashamed to admit that I missed most of these intimate, early morning sessions. An hour later, I would join him for a brisk walk around Rabindra Sarobar Lake, then return home for shower and breakfast. Throughout the day there would be numerous talk sessions, meeting with new people, perhaps undertake a sojourn to Santiniketan, go shopping, sightseeing or visit Guha's family in his ancestral home in Hind Motor. At least once during his stay, Guha would travel to Chandannagar, about 20 miles north of Kolkata, to meet friends. We, like little ducklings, would follow close behind. Situated on the banks of the Ganges, Chandannagar is a former French colony with its own unique cultural stamp. We would be home by 8 pm, have light dinner and chitchat with him or listen to a friend croon soulfully until about an hour later he would shoo us out. Through all these activities it is important to remember that Guha's presence was all that we craved, no matter where we were or what we were doing. That must be the reason why there is a clamor to sit on the sofa next to him or vie to be with him in the same car. Ever so often an amusing spectacle is sure to take place as someone or the other throws a fit of tantrum on being shunted to another vehicle. After all, there are only so many seats in a car. There is a strange pull which I am unable to comprehend that draws us to him like a moth to a flame.

Guha is spry and nimble for his age and can do five miles without blinking an eyelid. At least one vigorous walk a day is always on the agenda and that is one of the prime reasons why he always chooses his locations where there is ample space to walk. In Kolkata, he usually camps in the Ballygunge area (one of the most affluent localities in south city) with the lake just a stone's throw away. The pathways around this manmade waterbody are shaded by tall trees, and indeed it is pleasant to walk there in the mornings. In New Jersey, during winter months we go mall walking while in summer, strolls along the canal, in meadows, parks or gardens are in order.

The EC which ushered in so many "good" changes was also making me tear my hair out with a deeply personal issue. To dig out and confront again the pain and hurt, something I'd rather lock up in my heart and throw away the key has been excruciating. It's a mystery why I keep making fatal mistakes but when the winds of change are blowing the rubbish must be swept away. Guha upholds that one must never act cowardly and meekly let go of what is rightfully yours. He has always emphasized, "We have no choice but to address social issues and needs. Fortunately, we also have the capacity and the strength to address these needs." So be it.

On the subject of EC, Guha alludes to U.G.'s proximity for physiological changes in himself. In his talks, he admits his system began to respond to U.G. in a core, innate way, leading to a kind of "radical transformation" which obliterated the old way of thinking and living for good. Guha believes this was due to his intense love for U.G. which validates U.G.'s oft-repeated statement that attraction is the action. In *14 Days with U.G. in Palm Springs* (Bengali) Guha writes, "From the very first day that I came in touch with U.G., many physical and mental changes have been taking place. Consequently, the body mind influence has been creating many novel, strange experiences.... It excites me to think that it is possible for our spiritual evolution to have a simple straight cause which is physical transformation. This matter has such extraordinary significance that even to think of it gives me the goosebumps..."

On a different dimension, Guha's creative expression blossomed too. In *Road to Insanity* he declares, "The relationship I had with U.G. at that time was mysterious.... My energy was intense, and I could work for eighteen hours at a stretch. I was a powerhouse – I worked hard in my physics lab all day, and back home when I couldn't sleep at night I used to write. My condition at that time was that the 'me'– before losing its ground – wanted to create havoc, play every trick of the trade and entice me in every possible way to instill fear and pain to postpone its own demise. In so doing, my brain was continually throwing up things. I kept on writing, singing Bengali songs, studying biology, etc...." While in Palm Springs with U.G for the first time in 1996, Guha began jotting down his experiences in a diary which was published many years later as *14 Days with U.G. in Palm Springs.* Furthermore, he translated into Bengali, Mahesh Bhatt's biography *U.G. Krishnamurti: A Life* as well as *A Taste of Death* and penned numerous Bengali poems. I hope all his works are translated into English someday. Perhaps I must take the initiative...

Getting back to the present, I am at Manoj's, sipping delicious filter coffee made by Vidya. We are in a lazy mood, watching Guha chatting, texting with perplexed souls around the globe. As soon as he put the phone aside Sanjay immediately engaged him in a full-blown discussion on gurus, meditation and spiritual experiences. But am I even listening? I'm so wrapped up in my own thoughts and ideations that nothing can penetrate that dense fog. I give up but catch a gem:
Sanjay: "In meditation what do you see?"
Guha: "You can only see what you know. Feeling vital is very different from feeling a high in meditation." He adds after a pause, "As long as you depend on anybody else (gurus), you will be taken for a ride."

Sanjay arrived here last morning from New Delhi. He is a very busy lawyer but managed to take a few days off to make Guha's acquaintance. I imagined him to be pushy and brash but to my pleasant surprise he is quiet, affable and soft-spoken. He was a follower of Jiddu Krishnamurti for decades and even today continues to organize weekly meetings for JK fans. He heard of Guha recently from Manoj, an erstwhile JK enthusiast, and Kamal, the Air India pilot. He was fortunate to meet U.G. too a couple of times. Wonder how he finds Guha and his tribe.

March 1, 2015

This morning we cut our walk short and head to the airport to receive Kamal. The veteran pilot and a lifelong follower of U.G., is a close friend of Guha too for the last 20 years. He is on vacation and wants to spend it here with Guha. On our way, Julie is in an unusually communicative mood and is regaling us with U.G. tales. I have noticed that whenever Julie talks about U.G. she has a peculiar, faraway look on her face as if she wished she could go back in time and right all the wrongs. Often, there are tears in her eyes when U.G.'s name pops up. After being with her for months I realize her love for U.G. has not diminished one bit although he's been gone for years.

Once U.G. and Julie were at Penn Station, New York, when a stranger walked up to U.G. and said he loved the trousers U.G. was wearing. In response, U.G. told him to stay put and not budge from the spot, adding he would be right back. He quickly walked over to his hotel, which was close by, changed his pants, walked back to where the stranger was still waiting and handed over to him the trousers he had so admired.

On another occasion, U.G. and Julie were walking in Knightsbridge in London when suddenly U.G. emptied out his pockets and gave all the money to a panhandler who was begging on the street. Pleasantly surprised, the mendicant profusely thanked U.G. for his largesse, saying, "You are a good bloke." A few days later, they ran into the beggar again who immediately recognized U.G. Full of gratitude the man confessed that on account of receiving the generous bounty from U.G. money had started pouring in. He could not thank U.G. enough. U.G., in his customary way, did not say a word and quietly walked away.

We have reached the airport and are waiting outside to receive Kamal. His plane has already landed and being a small airport, he should be out any minute. Here he comes, with the ubiquitous backpack slung over his shoulders and dragging a small wheeler. A broad smile lights up his face when he spots us. Now I see him giving a bear hug to Guha, whom he calls "bade bhaiya" (elder brother). In turn, Guha calls him "Laxman bhaiya". So sweet! (In the ancient Sanskrit epic *Ramayana*, Laxman was the younger brother of Prince Rama.) Kamal's gregarious laughter is contagious and puts us in a jovial mood. Greetings over, he walks over to me and gives a polite handshake. On our way home, we halt at Kamal's hotel, and while he goes up to his room to freshen up, we treat ourselves to some refreshments in the restaurant.

I met Kamal for the first time in New York about a year ago. Luckily, it was a holiday for me and I was keen to see the Ansonia "office" which I had heard so much about. Guha said this was a good opportunity for me to meet his "very close friend Kamal" who was in the city for a couple of days. Like me, Kamal was a follower of Ramana Maharshi till he met U.G. while in his early twenties. Thus, Guha thought we would enjoy reminiscing about our past spiritual affiliation. As a senior captain, Kamal flies his Boeing 777 into JFK at least once a month from New Delhi. Notwithstanding the jetlag and the exhaustion after a 15-hour flight, he usually dumps his luggage in his hotel room, freshens up and takes the first available subway to spend as much time with Guha as possible. Maybe it's my imagination but I think Guha too is fond of his bro. Anyway, when I was introduced to Kamal, I was a little awed because I had never conversed with a pilot before. However, his amiable disposition put me at ease and soon we were exchanging notes on Ramana and U.G. I quickly realized that he had a rich history with U.G. and made a mental note to learn more at a later date.

~

Chapter Three

A Pilot's Tale

There is no better relationship than friendship.
– Guha

Last evening, I managed to wean Kamal away from Guha for a short time and engage him in revealing more about the two most important men who have been instrumental in shaping his life. On a leisurely stroll along the water bank near home, the warm-hearted, intrepid flyer opened up about his close association with U.G. Krishnamurti and an intimate friendship with Guha. Having literally spent his entire life chasing U.G., he now pursues Guha with the same intensity, fighting chronic sleep deprivation and fatigue. I find his perseverance and dedication truly commendable. Perhaps Kamal inherited his calling from his erstwhile father, who was a sincere seeker and later became a follower of Ramana Maharshi. He was also fond of discussing metaphysical matters with his youngest son Kamal although he never made U.G.'s acquaintance. However, Kamal's sister Anu and brother Ravi both were fortunate to meet U.G. several times. Anu who is adept at I Ching and astrology was even invited by U.G. to read his astrological chart. U.G., who loved indulging astrologers, palmists and Tarot experts, was appreciative of her talents and confided as much to Kamal.

Kamal, a diehard U.G. follower for almost 20 years surprisingly took to Guha like fish to water which he readily admits without any hesitation or reservations, "Even though U.G. was the only person who could read what was going on inside me - he was beyond ultra-sensitive - I find that kind of sensitivity in Guha too. U.G. meant the world to me but he never allowed me to associate with him as though he was an individual different from you and me. With Guha I feel the same way and I also find a core, deep connection with him. It is as if U.G.'s essence is reflected in Guha and U.G. has passed on the baton to Guha who is now my best friend, philosopher, guide and mentor. Out of affection he calls me chota bhaiya (younger brother) and I honor that with utmost gratitude."

Kamal continues, "My relationship with Guha is as intense as it was with U.G., so much so that I even find my body resonating perfectly in his proximity. I think of him as my big brother whose only concern is my well-being. Most people I know may be experiencing the same in his presence." Pointing to a small fishing vessel, he adds, "It's as if I am floating in a rudderless boat, going with the flow, heading nowhere but happy to be in the presence of my elder brother Guhaji."

Kamal was inexplicably drawn to Guha and his family early on. He reminisces, "Whenever I went to meet U.G., Guha, his wife Lakshmi and their two little girls would also be there and slowly, over time, a close friendship developed between us. I used to play with the girls, fly kites with them in Switzerland while Lakshmi, who is very industrious, would invariably be cooking for us, knitting or keep herself occupied with other chores. Guha, of course, would not budge from U.G.'s side. I was introduced to Guha when I went to see U.G. in New York in 1995. In fact, when U.G. offered him a ride to his home in New Jersey, I too accompanied them in the car. As usual, Julie was gracious to do all the driving. This was the first time U.G. and I went to Guha's house but did not go inside since U.G., who did not want to disturb Lakshmi, had forbidden Guha to tell her we were coming."

Kamal and Julie go a long way too, since both came under U.G.'s ambit in 1989. Kamal is the same age as Julie's youngest son and watching them together it is easy to discern that they share immense affection for each other. Kamal narrated an amusing incident which took place in Los Angeles, California, in 1991. He was undergoing training to get his commercial pilot's license when he learnt that U.G. was in San Francisco, about 400 miles away. For a pilot, what better option than to pay a flying visit to his mentor? He took a few days off and renting a single-engine, two-seater Cessna, flew into Novato airport where Julie was waiting to receive him. Kamal enthusiastically offered to take her on a joy ride but Julie, after one look at the "toy" plane quickly declined the invitation. Later, when I prodded her, she laughingly admitted, "I hate heights and the thought of flying in that little thing was horrifying. Moreover, Kamal was just a kid training to be a pilot and I would not fly with him then for dear life! But now if he asked me, probably I would acquiesce."

As a child, Kamal was intrigued listening to his parents discussing religion, meditation, experiences, etc. and became determined to find "god". In his quest, the nine-year-old walked five kilometers through wheat fields in scorching heat, with no water to get mantra diksha from a Sikh guru. As a teenager, he accompanied his family to Tiruvannamalai a few times where they were put up at Ramanasram guest house. Later, he continued to visit the sage's abode on his own and in course of time, began to practice self-enquiry, as advocated by Ramana. He joined the Army after graduating high school but his visits to the ashram continued. In the company of staunch old timers like Kunju Swami, Annamalai Swami and Rhoda McIver, Kamal was greatly inspired by their faith and devotion to their guru. He would occasionally climb up the Arunachala Hill with them to visit Virupaksha Cave or Skandasram where Ramana lived for many years. He spent long hours meditating and practicing self-enquiry in front of the sage's portrait on the sofa in the Old Hall where the wise man of Arunachala used to recline. The Old Hall was converted into a meditation room after his demise in 1950. The routine continued till Kamal was about 23 years old when a strange quirk of fate ended his mission abruptly.

Kamal continues, "When I was not meditating, I would be in the ashram library, reading and discussing stuff with the librarian who was a good friend of mine. One day, he threw a book on the table in front of me and commanded, 'Read this!' It was none other than the *Mystique of Enlightenment,* which I later termed 'a rebel of a book'. The minute I started reading it, I could not put it down, it was as if at the back of my mind I knew something calamitous had happened but could not put a finger on it. I finished reading the book from cover to cover then and there. That night when I went to bed, I was shivering and distinctly felt as if U.G. was trying to choke me to death. I got up with a jolt and was still trembling, but the book wouldn't leave me; I had to read it again. U.G had had turned every single ideation about god, guru, tradition, religion, spirituality on its head, in turn, creating chaos in my head! By now, I knew I had to meet this firebrand 'non-guru'. A few weeks later, I was sitting in front of U.G. in Bangalore."

Meeting U.G. was the singular most defining moment of Kamal's life that he would cherish forever. Looking at U.G., he intuitively knew that he was face to face with the guru he had been looking for, even though he was aware that U.G. despised that title. Says Kamal, "When I set my eyes on U.G. for the first time in Poorna Kuti I was in a daze and approached him with trepidation as well as hope. I had aspirations that as soon as U.G.'s gaze fell on me I would be enlightened. I was arrogant to think that I had practiced enough self-enquiry and was at the threshold of self-realization. I thought I would be enlightened instantaneously when encountering a real spiritual giant like U.G. But I was also anxious at the same time because I was entering unchartered territory and didn't know which way I would go from that point onwards. Just as Ramana had walked out of his home after his 'death' experience, perhaps it would be the same for me too. In fact, before going to meet U.G., I had even forewarned my father, 'Be prepared. I may not return home as a son to you.' I was so willing to be a copycat, as U.G. would have said.

"From the word go, U.G. began to debunk self-enquiry and asserted if there was anything to it, I would not be sitting in front of him. What he said was absolutely correct as I was practicing self-enquiry with an objective that had to be accomplished, i.e. a 'state' to be achieved. As this realization sank in, I was shattered but could not doubt his words. In despair, I questioned him relentlessly that there must be a way to achieve self-realization. Finally, one day U.G. told me sharply, 'GIVE UP!' There was such force and conviction in his voice when he told me to give up that my whole being accepted his words without further doubts. And I again instinctively knew in my heart that he was my guru and wanted to touch his feet as a mark of reverence. So, on the pretext of picking up coins which had fallen on the ground from my pocket, I bent down and touched his feet before he had time to react. I then immediately took his leave as I was heading to Mysore. After a couple of days on my return, I went to meet him again. As I was approaching the bungalow, from a distance I saw U.G. standing at the doorstep in a kurta-pajama as though he was waiting for someone. By the time I entered the main gate, he had already gone inside. It is my belief that he was waiting for someone (may be me) to arrive."

Kamal's second meeting proved to be very interesting as U.G. helped him clear doubts about his career path in his own inimitable way. He was having serious misgivings about continuing serving in the Army, and wanted to quit and become a commercial pilot instead. But before he took this important decision he wanted to discuss the matter with U.G. He elaborates, "While I was talking about this issue with U.G., Major Dakshinamurti, a patriotic Army-man (retired), a traditionalist and a hardcore U.G. votary, was also present. He was very keen that I should continue in the Army and encouraged me thus, 'It is such a noble profession and gives you the opportunity to defend our motherland, Bharat Varsham.' Before I could reply, U.G. (looking at me) retorted, 'No, sir! Please quit the Army. This country is not worth defending!' I took U.G.'s words as an endorsement in my aim to become a pilot although I have utmost respect for my country. Within a year after this talk I was discharged from the Army. Later, while undergoing training for a commercial pilot's license in California, I went to meet U.G. who was in San Francisco at the time. As soon as I entered the room, he exclaimed, 'Here comes the Air India pilot!' I laughed and replied, 'Sir, I have barely begun my training.' He merely smiled. Perhaps he knew where my future lay as I have been with Air India now for over 22 years."

After his second meeting with U.G., Kamal went back to Tiruvannamalai to gauge for himself if he felt the same or if things had changed vis-à-vis Ramana. Not surprisingly, this time thoughts about Ramana being his guru were totally absent. Thereafter, his visits to that place came to a stop.

Says Kamal, "U.G. was not just my master towards whom I had the utmost reverence, but he was also my best friend, guardian, philosopher, mentor, preceptor and guide. I joked with him like an intimate buddy and confided everything to him. We would chat about anything and everything, 'from disease to divinity, to use U.G.'s words but I never asked any questions on spiritual topics. That was because at the time I did not have any curiosity or have any burning questions for him. Over the next 17 years, I would visit U.G. wherever he called me - Switzerland, London, Australia, New York, California and of course, India. I think he enjoyed my company as much as I enjoyed meeting him. Till the day he died I considered him the only man known to me with whom I could relate intensely, yet with ease, even without much verbal communication. Once I told him, 'U.G., you are the ultimate guru! There is no one like you.' U.G. retorted, 'Is that so? Would you say that even if I cheated you?' I shot back, 'Try it, U.G.!' My relationship with him was such that I could joke with him as with any ordinary friend."

He continues, "While in the Army, I was once stationed in the Kumaon region in the Himalayas. Immediately upon reaching there, I called U.G. to declare my intention of living here in the mountains. In fact, I had already identified a plot of land where I could make a dwelling for myself. I told him, 'U.G., I am going to build a hut and live here.' But U.G. would hear none of it and interrupted me, 'No, sir! I'd rather you live in New York than in the Himalayas!' His words were not in vain as I have been traveling frequently to New York for many years to meet Guha, my learned mentor and brother. As soon as I heard U.G.'s dissuasion, all thoughts of living in the Himalayas vanished. His words were like gospel to me.

"On another occasion, U.G. was on an Air India flight from Singapore to Mumbai in which I was the first officer and the captain was an ardent JK follower. In the cockpit, both of us embarked on a heated argument about the philosophical differences between JK and U.G. with me passionately upholding U.G. philosophy and the captain strongly defending JK ideology. While keeping an eye on the control panel, we continued with the spirited debate, neither of us willing to accept defeat. By now the destination airport was in sight and the plane had begun its descent, when I suddenly noticed that the nose wheel of the landing gear had not deployed fully. I immediately alerted the captain who aborted the landing in the nick of time! The plane took off again, to land safely a little later. Later, U.G. confronted me, 'That was a close call, mister!' Utterly surprised, I asked him, "How did you know? We did not make any public announcement." U.G. retorted, "I have been flying since before you were born! After this incident, he made it a point to announce when I was there, "He almost killed me!" while narrating the whole incident.

"Once when I went to meet U.G. in Bangalore, Larry Morris, a very close friend of U.G. was also visiting. Larry is a minster in a church in New Mexico, US, and his devotion to U.G. is legendary. U.G. was in a ferocious mood, vehemently criticizing India, Indian values, traditions, etc. Larry and I, sitting quietly beside U.G. would dare not interrupt. But after a while, Larry mustered up courage and pointing to me, demanded, "U.G., what about this guy? He's Indian, isn't he? Do you hate him too?" Brushing off Larry's remark, U.G. replied nonchalantly, 'Oh, forget him! He's international, he doesn't count!'

"Talking about Bangalore, another story comes to mind. U.G. was in a room packed with people and when he saw me enter, he gestured to me to sit next to him on the sofa. A lady was singing *Guru Brahma, Guru Vishnu....* and everybody was listening raptly to her devotional outpouring. Suddenly, U.G. put his hand over mine which was by his side. Hiding my surprise, I adroitly turned my hand over in such a way that we were holding hands. Meanwhile, my throat got choked up and tears started pouring down my cheeks at U.G.'s love and compassion towards me. Just then the recitation ended, and someone suggested I should sing *Rhinestone Cowboy*. This is my signature song which I'm always asked to sing in gatherings. But today I just shook my head in a daze and U.G., my savior, came to my rescue saying, 'He will not be able to sing today.'"

Kamal was so attuned to U.G. that he could not bear to think of life without him. Once in 2005, he got up in the middle of the night with a distinct thud in his heart and was anguished at the thought that U.G. was no more! Overcome with grief, he called U.G. first thing in the morning and was relieved and happy when U.G. greeted him with, "I am alive and kicking! How're you?" Kamal continued meeting U.G. until mid-2006 when his pilot upgrade training was to have begun in Mumbai. However, it kept getting postponed sine die, preventing him from traveling to see U.G. Says Kamal, "By this time U.G. was in Europe, moving from place to place with friends. When I called Julie to wish her on her birthday that September, U.G. came on the line and straightaway asked, 'Mister, when is your training going to start?' While lamenting that it may be delayed even further, I was alarmed when he exclaimed, 'Oh my god!' My heart sank at his response, he sounded so ominous. Perhaps he sensed that I may never ever see him again.

"The training, which typically lasts for about six months, finally got underway in February 2007 so there was no question my going anywhere in the coming months. By now, U.G. was already in Vallecrosia, Italy, his final stop and his health was rapidly deteriorating. Alas, I was like a bird trapped in a cage, unable to fly to Italy and pay my last respects to my beloved master. The best I could do was meet Mahesh Bhatt, who was leaving for Vallecrosia the next day, and request him to personally convey my last "namaskarams" to U.G. My close friend Suresh, also an avid U.G. follower, accompanied me. I handed over a couple of CDs to Mahesh for U.G. I was told later that U.G. had listened very intently to the *Rudram Namakam Chamakam* and *Aditya Hridayam* CDs which I had especially bought for him.

"I spoke to U.G. for the very last time about two weeks before he passed away. In a shaky voice, I told him, 'U.G., I will always remember your words. I am privileged to have known you. You have been a friend, philosopher and guide to me and I will always cherish this association.' Later, Chandrashekhar Babu, who was by U.G.'s side, told me that when I called, U.G. had me on speaker phone and while I was talking, he made a gesture with his hands acknowledging my heartfelt valediction. Although I could not visit U.G. on his deathbed, my system was so hardwired to U.G. that I could withstand the disappointment, though unbearable at times. I always considered him to be a part of me and I feel his presence even today in everything I do. The same energy in its sublime purity has taken a different form and continues to express its beneficent presence in my life."

~

Chapter Four

Sense of Self

We as we know ourselves are created by the fakeness of our culture. The status quo wants you to function in a way that is in conflict with the system. Your imagination is always making you see things the way they are not.
– Guha

March 2, 2015

- *There is no such thing as silence. Tell me one word about silence. You can say absence of sound. Is that the definition? There will never be "absence of sound" unless you are asleep and don't know what you are hearing. Or, you are incapable of paying attention to what is hammering your eardrums. You are always thinking, so there is no silence.*
- *The sense of self is created out of an external authority and that authority operates in fear. If suddenly that fear goes, all the authority that is established inside you, knowingly or unknowingly, also goes.*
- *Human thinking has given you power and the misuse of power is the cause of all this – this I call the 'disorder of the sense of self'.*
- *The sense of self is so important, but it doesn't exist. You cannot locate it in your brain. No scientist can ever locate it – it is a total operation of the brain structure itself.*

- *If somebody made you believe that you can reduce your sense of self to zero, you are going to be on a wild ride all your life and become frustrated because the instrument measuring IS the sense of self. So, you will never know if the sense of self has become zero – not a possibility. Either by inflating your sense of self or trying to reduce it to zero, you are falsifying yourself.*
- *If somebody says they are in a state of Advaita, they are telling you a bullshit story. It's not possible, because the instrument they are using to think they are in the Advaita state is the same instrument that is in existence because of duality. The information that you gather and is stored as memory in human species, if that is not there you are a vegetable.*
- *I feel that there is energy inside us which makes us what we are. Mother Nature has given us so much and we are so resilient, so powerful that no matter how much we torture ourselves, it still forgives us and the next morning allows us to go through the same junk all over again.*
- *With no oxygen in your head you cannot think at all. The prime mover is the one who is operating inside us and 97.5% of the activities are absolutely automatic (parasympathetic). It does its job because it is perfect. It's not like our thoughts. You can have wrong thoughts but heartbeat, no chance – if it misses, you are out! It is perfect. It is running by the tinkering of millions of years of intelligence of Mother Nature and allowing you to do whatever and you think you are running the show; it's the other way around. No action can take place inside without reaching the information bank and that is the first doorway to human interaction.*

  – Guha

In the last quote Guha mentioned that most of our body functions are automatic. This reminds me of what he said in *Dangerous to Ponder*, "*The connectivity of life is so complicated that it bypasses much of our intellectual ground and recognition processes that are accessible to self-consciousness. Our brain's limbic system is where most of the functions and relay processing take place. It makes one feel like there is a guy sitting there in the thalamus. Well, not a guy really, but many nuclei!* This passage is somehow stuck in my head and I come back to it again and again to marvel at its import. In fact, when I was reading it for the first time, I felt as if my brain had frozen and I was in a swoon. I again recall Guha, *you are nothing but a conglomeration of fictitious desires. Everything in you is put in you systematically by culture. Nandini is not real! Nandini is a fictional entity! Because there is no Nandini how can she create demands? What she feels, demands, everything, it is fictitious.*

After a brief, head-spinning daybreak session we disperse to get ready as we are embarking on a long road trip. We are headed to Kanyakumari, the southernmost point of the Indian sub-continent. It is only about 300 km from Cochin but will take eight hours to cover. If we start soon, by late afternoon we should be in the beach town of Kovalam, about two-thirds of the way. Located near Kerala's capital Trivandrum, it is a popular tourist site and I have been dreaming of visiting it for many years. Our plan is to have lunch there and resume the drive till we get to Kanyakumari before sunset. We will return to Kovalam for the night where Manoj has already booked us hotel rooms.

After the usual chaos and confusion as to who travels with Guha, we settle into two cars and are on our way. Guha is in top form and when I ask him the secret behind his ever-ebullient disposition, he jests, "Some people can't stand that I'm happy all the time." As I wonder at how light it feels to be in his energy field, I must warn that he is not always so easy going. Some of us know very well that Guha can make you squirm when he puts you in the "hot seat" and ruthlessly tears apart your most cherished notions or trashes your idols. Oh, and I shudder to think of being at the receiving end of his "perturbation tactics"; the disturbances he creates are so painful that you are ready to jump off a cliff.

The weather is pleasant right now with a soft breeze blowing but it promises to be a hot day. As I look out of the car window, the city of Cochin or Kochi, is humming with life and traffic is already building up. We slowly wind our way through the morning rush hour to eventually arrive at the outskirts of the town. Soon the driver pulls into the parking lot of a popular restaurant serving traditional south Indian breakfast. As we stretch our legs, Guha's devil-may-care, contagious laughter puts us in a cheerful mood. The bustling roadside eatery is doing brisk business as a steady stream of office-goers, college students and laborers, many in traditional *lungis,* stop by to grab a quick bite. Meanwhile, the *muttaśśis* and *muttacchans* (grandmothers and grandfathers) are in no rush, leisurely sipping their coffee as they ponderously study the newspaper and catch up on the day's gossip. We enjoy a hearty meal of idli/dosa/vadai - steamed cake, crepe and fried savory donut respectively. The first two are made from a combination of lentil-rice fermented batter while vadai consists solely of lentil batter. All are served with delicious coconut chutney and vegetable curry. Satiated, we down it with hot filter coffee, the best coffee in the world, and hit the road again.

I am traveling in a big, comfy SUV with Guha sitting next to the driver in the front, I in the middle, flanked by Julie and Kamal while Sanjiv and Bubu are in the rear. To my right is Julie, sometimes dozing off, sometimes snapping photos with her phone and sending them to R & R and other overseas friends at their request. To my left is Kamal, who looks tired but is in a jolly frame of mind. Every now and then I see his head bobbing up and down as he tries to catch a few winks. He reminds me of a poster I saw somewhere for pilots which read 'Eat, Sleep, Fly Repeat'. Seriously, for pilots who crisscross the continents as often as Kamal does, living with a messed up circadian rhythm and chronic fatigue must be tough on themselves as well as their families.

The drive is delightful as we pass through palm-fringed back waters with abundant greenery all around. Apart from being blessed with diverse geographical landscapes ranging from unspoiled beaches, lush back water lagoons and exotic highland plantations, the 'God's own country' is also famous for its extravagant spa clinics, Ayurvedic resorts, five-star yoga retreats, unique art forms and much more. Those seeking natural remedies for chronic ailments, "Panchkarma" is very popular and widely prescribed here. Ayurveda's "Panchkarma", meaning five cleansing therapies, is an ancient treatment formulated to flush out toxins from the body which cause disease or discomfort. With so much to offer, it is little wonder that tourists of all shades, including eco-tourists, culture aficionados and beach lovers from every corner of the world flock to this little paradise in droves.

I am jolted out of my reverie to hear Guha rail against the value system, ".... That whole thing was knocked out of me. I don't give a shit about the greatest of the great people. They are by themselves individuals, and so am I. It showed me that it is impossible for me to be like anybody and, in fact, I don't need to be like anybody. The system is complete by itself and doing everything it can do. All the praises, criticisms become meaningless.

"We don't value ourselves. Just a miniscule, honest reflection should show you that the instrument you are using to exemplify somebody is a small part of this fascinating machine that is making it work, the body, which you regard as nothing. It's like a camera which produces a beautiful picture, and you are completely taken in by the picture but never value the camera, or the amount of work that went in to produce such things. The human body is working for itself, by itself and is part of nature and no matter how much you try you can never be sure how it came. The body moves in a way that every second it knows how to protect itself. We might create model after model and be completely convinced about them, but you are still not sure about yourself. Anybody who has any intelligence can immediately find out and will be so humbled that he can never be part of this machine. It is the working of the machine that is producing his ideas; he is a foreigner there.

"That appreciation (of others) is created out of a very different set of dynamics called the status quo. Actually and factually, it is not for its own sake. Any small amount of thinking can show you that you can never be like anybody else. To be like someone is a foolish idea because you do not know who or what you are, leave alone to try to change into something else. How stupid! You have no idea what you are dealing with and want to reshape it to acquire peace or be like somebody. It has no meaning, as far as I am concerned. My talking to you is like quicksilver; you say yes, yes, yes and the next second you will go back thinking the same way. You will never, ever say 'this is it.'"

After the cloudburst, we sit quietly and dare not ask any more questions. I begin to reflect on my conversation with Guha last night. Seeing that I was somewhat listless and despondent, he looked me squarely in the eye and straightaway asked: "What do you want? Ask yourself, what is it that you really want?" He said to think hard and answer with utmost honesty. *What do I want?* That's a tough one, Guha, I am at a loss how to answer that. The more I contemplate on it the more it takes me on a merry-go-round. Is there anything I can truly call my own? My so-called wants, desires, aspirations and goals, including wanting self-enlightenment, have been subtly and not so subtly dictated by society right from childhood. *These are created by your will. They have been systematically introduced into you by social dynamics so that there is a relationship between you and society.* One thing is clear though that money or lack of it has always been a major cause for my so-called unhappiness and a painful reminder of times gone by.

Growing up in Mumbai was a mixed bag. On the one hand, I had a pretty ordinary childhood filled with school activities and happy playtimes with buddies. I remember running outside in pelting rain to sail paper boats in swirling drains or walk to the nearby Chowpatty beach to build sand castles and gather sea shells. On the other hand, my domestic situation was far from pretty and adolescence onwards, it got worse and worse. Our household consisted of ten members, eleven, if you count our live-in help, with me being the youngest of the clan. We all - my parents, elder brother, my uncle, who was my father's half-brother, aunt and their four children (my elder cousins) - lived cheek by jowl in a gloomy, ground floor flat in a middle-class neighborhood. Between us, we had to split three 'family' rooms, a kitchen and one teeny weeny bathroom admeasuring 4x4 feet. The dingy house was choc-o-bloc with oversized furniture, altars to various Hindu deities plus daily necessities and knickknacks of ten inmates. Sharing such cramped quarters with my next of kin for nearly 30 years was as easy as climbing Mount Everest. Persistent paucity of funds, lack of privacy and personality clashes galore gradually eroded any semblance of kinship, affinity or civility between us. Things came to a head when I was in my late twenties, forcing us to sell the house and go our own ways. Luckily, over the years, we mended fences and are closer than even before. Anyway, few months after the split I got married but no respite there either. It was like jumping from frying pan into the fire.

Till I finished high school, I shared a room either with my parents or other family members that was located at the back of the house, facing a one-storied decrepit building. It was occupied by poor, destitute families where cheap booze and petty crime flourished. In the compound of this rundown structure, a fat Christian woman lived with her brood and operated an illegal, country liquor bar. To hide the nefarious goings-on from prying eyes, a black canvas canopy was always in place, so luckily, we could not see what was happening there but could hear everything loud and clear all day and all night. Her customers included drivers, servants (ours included as he grew old), menial workers, fishermen from a nearby fishermen's colony, and cops too. The notorious bartender was known to ingratiate herself with the law enforcement by providing them with bootleg liquor free of charge but despite her efforts, the illicit, makeshift bar was raided many times by the police. However, as soon as it was destroyed, and the tarp pulled down, a new one went up instantly with help from her honchos. Often, fights erupted between her and her inebriated clients over payment and she would yell and hurl choice abuses at them. Sometimes we even heard a resounding whack as she gave a wayward client the taste of a hard punch on the face. Thus, my childhood memories are full of the witch screaming until her voice went hoarse, and her babies wailing their lungs out, perhaps out of fright.

Guha says money is like oxygen in social dynamics and whenever I am reminded of my life in that house, I could not agree more. With money, my father could have moved out years earlier and provided us with a better home, a better life. With money, my mother could have gone to college, which was her ambition. With money, my family could have sent me to an elite boarding school, which was my dream. Living away from home would have been a perfect solution to my woes. It would have bolstered my self-confidence big time, helping me cultivate a positive self-image and equip me to face life on my own terms. By trusting my inner strength and resilience, I could have chalked out a different life-path for myself instead of cowering in fear and suffering in silence when injustices were heaped on me. Oh well, time to knock it off, and let bygones be bygones. Today, I am fortunate to be here with this miracle named Guha around whom healing happens effortlessly, where the emotional scars left behind from those long, traumatic years are beginning to fade away.

Money remains an issue even today where I am still stressed about landing a job and paying off big loans. But I can already discern a hazy rainbow in cloudy skies growing vivid by the minute and if I make a wish now to travel with Guha carefree and "money-worry-free", the universe will have to grant it. So, to come back to the original question, *what do I want*, my answer in the most practical terms is, money. But I found love too without asking!

We are at Kovalam beach near our hotel which is not that big but looks clean and inviting. The red and white Vizhinjam lighthouse stands tall amidst the palm trees at one end, its beacon of light proudly guiding seamen since the 70s. The afternoon scorching heat does not seem to ruffle the hordes of foreign tourists as they chat amiably with local folk, sipping cold beverages in open shack-like eateries lining the boardwalk. Many prefer to lounge under colorful umbrellas while some brave the harsh sun to acquire a tan. I find it amusing that while Indians have a fetish for "white skin", the "goras" are always looking to "brown" themselves. However, we have no time to linger as we must be on the road again to reach our target in time otherwise the whole endeavor would be in vain.

We quickly check in to our hotel rooms, freshen up, have a hurried lunch in one of the shacks and get into our cars again. Driving through overcrowded villages and towns slow us down considerably and we urge the driver to take the highway, but this tall, well-built Malayali will not be swayed by our demands. He is content to drive on congested roads instead of the obvious choice of taking bypasses and freeways. When Guha finally asked him to hasten, the fellow replied in dead earnest that the highway was not an option as far as he was concerned because he would be tempted to speed and may end up getting a speeding ticket. The entire exercise was due to his fear of being fined about Rs 200 which is less than three dollars. However, despite frustrating delays, here we are.

Kanyakumari gets its name from the ancient temple dedicated to goddess Kumari Amman where she is worshipped as a young girl or kanya. The coastal town lies in the state of Tamil Nadu but is easily accessible from neighboring Kerala as well. The country's Land's End offers spectacular views of sunrises and sunsets over waters where the Arabian Sea, the Bay of Bengal and the Indian Ocean converge. At certain times, sitting in the same spot surrounded by three waters on three sides, you can view all three – sunrise, sunset and moonrise – on the same day. Isn't that magical? Around full moon you can also view sunset and moonrise at the same time. According to Hindus, bathing at the confluence is a sacred rite and their duty which supposedly washes away all sins. Did I hear Guha smirk? Debunking this age-old myth, he declares, “If you think bathing in these waters will get rid of your sins, good luck to you. If that were so, the world would be a very different place.” Kamal is the only one amongst us who takes a dip in the “holy” water trine. He says such an opportunity may never arise again. This place is also an important pilgrim center where people from all walks of life come to pay their respects to Swami Vivekananda, the beloved monk of the Ramakrishna Order. The rock memorial, where the swami is said to have attained enlightenment, attracts thousands of visitors every month.

Just as the sun is beginning to set we race to the beach which has a distinctly rocky shoreline with giant black stones stretching into the ocean. Some of us stop to have a quick cup of *chai* from a vendor but it is tepid and tasteless. The sea shore is jam-packed with swarms of people milling about, the ubiquitous beggars running after tourists and the ever-present hawkers enticing little ones with toys and balloons, hoping their parents will buy their wares. In the melee, I get separated from others and get nervous when I am unable to find a familiar face among the sea of people. Thankfully, after a few tense minutes I locate Guha standing on a rock at a distance and sprint up to him before I lose him again. From now on I stick to him for dear life. I remove my flip-flops and alongside others, gingerly hop from boulder to boulder to get to the furthermost rocky outcrop. Now it is just me and the mighty sea, nothing in-between. Water, water everywhere, as far as the eyes can see with the orange orb in the distant horizon engulfing us in a golden, almost supernatural light. I stare mesmerized at the reflection of the setting sun in the dancing waters creating mystical, flame-colored patterns. Mother Nature has put on a spectacular show and I bow my head in silent homage.

All around spectators are busy taking photos and videos, trying to capture the enchanting twilight moments. Julie and Vidya too managed to record the entire phenomenon on their smartphones. Before the sun disappears into the ocean, we pose for one last group photo. People have already begun to disperse as night falls swiftly. We too exit the beach and find a café where they serve us authentic ginger chai. We are gratified that our mission has been accomplished. Like U.G., we can now proudly proclaim, "Been there, done that."

It is late night by the time we are back in Kovalam. Guha, Julie and others are too tired to eat dinner and retire to their rooms immediately. I am ready to drop too but need hot food in my belly first, so along with Kamal and Kishor, head out to hunt for a diner which is still open at this hour. We trudge alongside the beach listening to the waves gently lapping against the shore, and after about half an hour arrive at a place just about to close. Reluctantly, they agree to serve us dal rice and after an agonizing 45-minute wait, we gorge on a hot meal. Now with a little more strength in my legs, I plod back to the hotel around midnight, bone-tired but content. I am delighted with the room arrangement and after a hot shower, snuggle into bed. Sweet dreams!

Next morning, we are up early and get ready for a walk in the sands before we start for home. The sun is shining bright and it is already warm and sticky. Kishor and I are taking it slow as others easily outpace us. We strike up a conversation and decide to sit on shaded steps leading to the beach till others return. He is a man of contrasts, unassuming but with a flair for drama, nonchalant but observing everything around him with sharp interest and mostly quiescent but with an ever-ready quip up his sleeve. His humorous one-liner jokes are a big hit with everyone, including Guha. Come to think of it, he did act in Gujarati plays years ago. Right now, though he is somberly narrating how he met Guha. As I listen to his spiritual thirst, first being with Ranjit Maharaj, then stumbling upon U.G. books and ultimately finding Guha, I am again reminded how fascinating and unique each one's spiritual journey is. Far away, I see Guha wading in the water with his trousers folded to his knees while Julie is merrily splashing in the waves with child-like abandon, completely impervious to her clothes getting soaked. I take a deep breath, enthralled once again looking at the boundless, unfathomable expanse in front of me.

Breakfast over, we pack our bags and are ready to depart. I am eager to see the Leela resort that I have heard so much about and which is not too far from our hotel. Guha kindly agrees to take the detour for my sake. The hotel is tastefully designed and blends perfectly with the surroundings. Perched on a cliff-top, it overlooks two pristine beaches on either side with sweeping views of the Kovalam coastline. Interestingly, the ocean appears a lovely azure blue from our vantage point and I believe this is the only spot where you can get to see this color of water here.

We leisurely explore the grounds and walk down to the private enclosed beach. I notice a swing hanging from a palm tree, made of thick coir rope and a wooden plank. It looks inviting and the swing freak that I am, I run, jump on it and like a pendulum swing to my heart's content. Julie, of course, gets active with her camera. Catching sight of Guha and friends near the exit, I make a dash towards them lest they leave me behind. Beaming at me, Guha laughs that he would have joined me on the swing, but I never invited him. Overjoyed I exclaim, "Why didn't you tell me earlier? Now I must take you back, until then we can't leave." In a buoyant mood I lead Guha to the same swing and gleefully pose sitting next to him. It endeared him to me even more. To be clear, Guha surely has no interest in sitting on a swing with me or anyone else, he is only reflecting our wishes. He has pointed out many times that it is just stimulus and response for him, not volitional on his part. But he sure made me a very happy lady that day. I will always cherish fond memories of the "swing leela" and other wondrous "leelas"[4] in this short but memorable excursion. I hope to come back here again someday with K.

---

3. The Sanskrit word "leela" has a special place in Hindu scriptures. It cannot be literally translated to English but can be loosely defined as "divine play" or "play".

Chapter Five

There Is No You

Some are of the opinion that I am a doomsday sayer, hopeless and negative, and you think that you are listening and feeling depressed. You feel that way because I am questioning the very foundation of your belief structure and the validity of the assumptions on which it is built. You don't have the courage and the patience to hear me through and examine this by yourself. If you do so, you may see your present situation in a different light.

– Guha

March 4, 2015

6.30 am

We returned home late last night, tired but full of good cheer. Come morning, we are up early and waiting for Guha, ready for a dynamic talk session. Like honeybees we want to extract as much nectar as we can from this wise man of Bengal:

- *You have to live within your conceptual freedom. Somebody is going to tell you what is good for you. Humans are the only species on the planet who do not know what to eat. Mein kya khaoon? Kya khaane se mera tabiyat theek rahega? (What should I eat? Which foods should I eat to keep good health?)*
- *You can't love another person because the one who loves, loves*

themselves. If you transcend that – if the need for you to love someone or to be loved by someone is gone, then you don't need love. In that condition you will never hurt someone. When you are truly, deeply concerned about another, there IS no you!

- *You cannot accept the unknowability of life, so you give solidity to what you believe is real and try to comfort yourself; that creates huge conflicts.*
- *You can struggle to get out of the pressure; the conflict is stifling you, but you cannot fix it. The minute you try to fix it, you make it worse. Volition is another way of creating another reality.*
- *The fact that I'm here is the only reality and (looking at Manoj) not because I accepted your invitation! Wanting to know how things happen is the mischief of the myth-making machine.*
- *All liquids expand when they are heated, except water which shrinks when heated (from 0 to 4 degrees Celsius). That's why there's always an exception to the rule.*
- *Thinking cannot produce the seamless universe which is in front of you.*
- *Every time you open your eyes the universe that is unfolding in front of you is like an image of several hundred terabytes of memory – a dense seamless, vibrant image with no gaps whatsoever, from almost infinity up to here, everywhere, it's just right there – a total compact full universe is unfolding. The sense that comes out of this reflection is so mind-boggling! The moment you close your eyes and try to remember what you have witnessed a different animal is born. What you know as Guha, Manoj or Nandini has begun trying to create a reality of its own out of fragments of memory.*
- *Basically, you as you know yourself are a slave of the social structure. They want you to be in the best mental and physical health so that you can be most productive. It's all business. Nobody gives a damn about you because you are a replaceable commodity.*

After bidding a fond farewell to the sea jewel Kovalam last

morning, we immediately hit the road for home. By the time we arrived at Kumarakom, just over 20 km from Cochin, it was already lunchtime and we were famished. Kamal has membership of a popular resort situated on the banks of the humungous Vembanad Lake and he had phoned them earlier to make lunch arrangements for our large group. As we approached the main reception area, the one-lane dirt road was quite treacherous with marshy ditches on both sides. However, once inside, we were in the midst of sylvan surroundings. Underneath tall trees, cozy guest cottages were aesthetically placed, with some perched prettily on stilts overlooking the backwaters while others faced the lake. Miniature arched bridges, winding trails, rustic wooden benches and pathways flanked by bright flowerbeds made the place look like a scenic wonderland.

Perhaps Kumarakom takes the top spot for backwater tourism in Kerala with its biggest lake drawing thousands of visitors every month. Plus, the nearby 14-acre bird sanctuary is a major attraction too. But as we all know, everything comes with a price and Kumarakom is no exception. With the proliferation of world class resorts and the flourishing of houseboat tours offering the quintessential Kerala experience of exploring the backwaters in these floating palaces, the entire Vembanad Lake region is being adversely impacted. Sadly, it is one of the most polluted lakes in the world today with the region's fragile eco-system in great peril. Guha has asserted time and again that man wants to control and manipulate everything in Nature for his own selfish gains and wish fulfillment.

After a big buffet lunch, we decided to digest all that rich food by taking a stroll in the well-kept gardens. While Manoj and Vidya retired to the office area to make important phone calls, the rest of us were content to wander about aimlessly. Kamal, Bubu, Sanjiv, Sanjay and Kishor forged ahead singing old, romantic Bollywood songs with great gusto while Julie, Guha and I followed at a leisurely pace enjoying the tranquil environs. Soon, we entered a coconut grove on one side of the restaurant and right there, in a shaded area, I spotted a lovely, ethnic "jhoola" (a swing in Hindi), as if waiting just for me. Perched on a wooden stand, it was covered with an overhead canopy, fitted with sturdy, ornate metal rails and could easily seat three people comfortably. I needed no further invitation.

The swing took me back to my ancestral village of Dakor in Gujarat where I spent many a summer during school vacations. My maternal grandparents had established themselves there since the late 1920s and were highly respected in the community. My grandfather, whom we called Dadaji was a doctor during British rule and after his retirement led a sedentary life dedicated to Lord Krishna. Dakor is home to the famous temple of Shri Ranchhodrai, a form of Krishna, dating back to 1772 and is a major pilgrim center. As family tales go, the lord himself had given my Dadaji a sign to put roots in Dakor. My grandpa was charismatic, gregarious, and a fantastic story-teller and every day there was a steady stream of visitors from morning till evening wanting to have "gup shup" (chit-chat) with "doctor sahib". Besides, although he had stopped practicing medicine long ago, patients with minor or chronic ailments inadvertently sought his advice. In fact, his "padiki" (a small, rectangular paper packet folded securely with a measured amount of medicinal powder inside) was very popular for curing headaches, migraines, nausea, even stomach cramps. He had concocted this pain-relieving mixture himself and handed it out to whoever requested it. Over time, the little packet became synonymous with the best pain medicine in town. He never charged anyone a penny till the day he died.

Dadaji and Ba (grandmother) had a penchant for "jhoolas" or "hinchkas", as they are called in Gujarati. They had two in their modest second floor home, one in the outer room and a bigger one, which looked more like a floating raft, in the bedroom. The raft was my favored one and it was on this that I recall taking naps with my head on my mother's lap while she sang devotional songs. Dakor was one getaway where mummy was likely to be in a relatively softer mood unlike in Mumbai where she tended to be belligerent in that oppressive atmosphere. In retrospect, the same goes for me too. It was on this raft that I cultivated love for reading. I would lie down for hours and get immersed in fairy tales, comic books, mythologies and text books. I would read the same stories over and over again till my eyes wore out. Incidentally, we carried our reading material from Mumbai as there was not a single library in Dakor at that time. Not sure if there's any now. I also did my summer homework on my special swing and play cards or "snakes and ladders" with my local friends. However, my best-loved sport was pretending that we were flying far, far away on the magic raft and giving the "hinchka" a powerful push, swing higher and higher till it was just a couple feet from the ceiling. Ba, on the verge of having a heart attack when she saw this spectacle would admonish us severely and force us to slow down. It made her nervous to think that if we got injured there was neither a hospital nearby nor provisions at home to treat serious injuries. Luckily, no one ever got hurt but it was a lot of fun for a little girl craving for adventure.

Every summer I looked forward to these visits because Dakor was the only place where I felt free as a bird and happy as a lark. This dirty, dusty village somehow awakened the daredevil in me and kindled my free spirit which was always camouflaged in Mumbai. Here I roamed the streets without any fear, wherever my heart desired, just like a gypsy. Sometimes, my feet would be covered with blisters wandering barefoot on hot, mucky roads littered with cow dung and trash, but I didn't care a hoot. I would be merrily slurping on colorful ice "golas" (crushed ice flavored with bright edible colors) or guzzling down ice-cold lemonade from wayside carts. I also loved to frolic with my girlfriends inside the big temple complex which was just a stone's throw away from our home. Thousands of devout folks from neighboring hamlets and towns come here every single day to worship the beloved black idol of Krishna. For hours together we would entertain ourselves playing hide and seek or hopscotch on white marble steps leading to the main viewing hall. At closing time, the temple guards would kindly escort me back home. Once in a while, the temple manager would summon my brother and me to his office and give us "prasad" and candy. He was a sweet, old gentleman who loved to hear about our life in Mumbai. Occasionally, on a pleasant evening, my mother would pull me out of the temple, dress me nicely and take me on a short boat ride on Gomti river to pay our respects at the Hanuman temple on the opposite bank. It was very peaceful here as hardly anyone came out this far. After spending half an hour or so in quietude we would return home walking or in a horse-drawn buggy, feeding cows in various cowsheds called *goshalas* on the way.

Apart from my outdoor capers, being with my granddad was very special. His joie de vivre was inexhaustible, and we were sucked into it in his presence. Dadaji loved children and children of all ages loved Dadaji. We would giggle uncontrollably watching him enact funny stories or be enthralled with his magic tricks, like when he materialized candy or trinkets out of thin air. Often, he would come out on the roof when we were flying kites and give us tips on how to be a super kite master. His youthful, lively spirit was very contagious and brought out playfulness in me too. I would stealthily slither up to his room while he was taking a nap in the afternoons and pull his cheeks till he woke up with a start. His eyes would fly open and seeing me he would pretend to be angry, mutter something under his breath and reach for a jar of candy next to his bed. After handing me my favorite orange peppermint, he would shoo me out.

Dadaji had a room to himself next to the terrace on top of the house. From that vantage point, we had wonderful views of the river and beyond from the netted window while the gentle breeze blowing ever so softly from the Gomti always put us in a mellow mood. Moreover, he was very fond of fragrant essential oils or attars and his room always smelled of rose petals or jasmine which kind of added to the surreal atmosphere. At sundown his friends would gather and they would chitchat for hours about… Krishna and his escapades, what else! My dear granddad died at the age of seventy-nine while I was still in high school. Thereafter, the house was locked up as Ba went to live with one of my aunts in another city which put an end to our visits. All these memories came flooding back when I saw the "jhoola" and will remain etched in my heart forever. After all, who am I if not my memories? As Guha says, "Man is nothing but memories. If memories go, YOU go."

Guha and Julie joined me on the swing with the rest of the gang surrounding us. As we sat there discussing mundane matters, Guha, out of the blue, decided we should go for a spin on the lake. Guha's wish was our command and soon a large motorboat materialized for our pleasure. The unexpected excursion put everyone in high spirits and we boarded the boat with loud cheers. Once everyone was settled in, we were zipping around the lake at dizzying speed. Kamal and Sanjay found two royal-looking, high-backed cane chairs in the middle and reclined on them like kings, while the rest of us sat around them like their subjects! Kamal was in a jovial mood, cracking jokes, sparring good naturedly with his buddy Manoj and narrating amusing anecdotes.

Without warning an ominous black cloud covered the sky and before we knew it, the heavens burst open and it started to rain heavily. Our well-trained boatmen quickly unfurled a massive canvas sheet on the bow to protect us from the lashing rain and wind. The greyish, weather-beaten tarpaulin swaying and flapping in the wind looked kind of artsy and Julie could not resist snapping away with her smartphone. Sitting by myself, staring pensively at the raindrops falling like sparkling diamonds on the heaving lake, my mood turned too as suddenly I felt intensely alone and alienated, even amidst all the revelry. This is not a new phenomenon to me as oddly I am often thrown out of whack in front of people. Perhaps, it is due to some strange conditioning where my inner balance is upset in certain situations. Will I ever be free of such a distressing (to myself) reaction? As the emotional storm raged within, the words of poet Samuel Coleridge flashed in the back of my mind:

"Alone, alone, all, all alone,
Alone on a wide, wide sea!
And never a saint took pity on
My soul in agony."

Guha seldom misses anything and I am sure he noticed my ashen face but thankfully kept quiet and did not embarrass me in front of others. He knows better than anyone else the machinations of our devious minds, but he also understands that at times it is best to allow people to come to grips with themselves, by themselves. I truly appreciate his sensitivity to such things. Later, though, he did enquire if I was okay. The rain stopped as abruptly as it had started, and the sun was again peeking through the clouds. After the jaunt, we stopped briefly at another well-known hotel for late tea and by the time we returned home it was already bedtime.

This morning, following a leisurely breakfast we amble over to Manoj's house. Guha is regaling us with humorous tales about a long-time friend who lives abroad. This continued for some time, after which Guha requested Sanjiv to sing a well-known devotional song to Krishna. It went something like why is Radha jealous when all are dear to Krishna and Krishna is dear to all? It so happened that while Sanjiv was singing, Guha received a call from Radhika in New Jersey. Listening to Guha bantering with her about the song, it struck me that just like Krishna's Radha, our Radhika is also so crazy after her Kanha (Guha) that she will readily jump off a cliff if he asked her to. Just for fun they're planning to send Sanjiv's recording to her. All just a good time pass. What else is there anyway?

March 5, 2015

I am determined to have a one-on-one talk with Guha today and after our morning walk I get my wish. My dejected frame of mind is again exposed as I ask the same old questions: Why is there so much pain and suffering in life? What does my future look like? How long will I remain jobless? How will I sustain myself? Should I sell my house? Will Parting Shot take off, which Julie and I am so keen to turn into a flourishing publishing house? Why do relationships have to be so painful? I don't want to get hurt again, yada, yada, yada…

Guha listens to my rant with full attention. Noticing tears rolling down my cheeks, he is very considerate as he gently points out that the pain is caused because of our inability to control life. He so wants to make me understand that life does not work according to the will of the myth-making structure - our sense of self which is trying in vain to capture life and use it the way it wills it to be. He patiently reiterates that the sense of self in me called Nandini is illusory. The identifier is also illusory. She is a conditioned organism which has been programmed to respond or react in the social context according to whatever has been systematically put into her since childhood. "They (people) put on a façade to run away from the pain. To capture life through words and images is impossible. That impossibility if it hits home will collapse the illusory structure on which Nandini is maintaining the status quo. That's an exercise in total futility."

He says Nandini is feeling uneasy because given the parameters there is no way of predicting the course her life will take in future. In that sense, future is continually created to control life. And to her that absence of hope for a happy future, i.e. the happiness she seeks according to her *samskaras* and conditioning, or the unknowability of knowing what's going to happen, makes her feel insecure and full of fear. "Right now, you are sitting here with me, but you are ignoring these precious moments by worrying about a future that only exists in your imagination." My heart missed a beat as I heard him say that in a matter-of-fact tone. I am ashamed to admit how true his words rang.

March 6, 2015

Finding me again despondent, Guha is more forceful, telling me I have zero satisfaction being with him. He adds with a wicked smile that I am like fish out of water writhing from pangs of separation, that I look and act like a love-lorn chick. "All relationships are fraught with pain and only fleeting pleasure," he adds for good measure. I reel under the unanticipated attack and struggle to defend myself. But he is in no mood to hear any of my tame excuses and walks out. I feel helpless and rudderless; where am I headed? As I try to compose myself, this realization arises from the depths of my consciousness, instantly lifting my spirits: *There is no future, there is no relationship, there is no love. Therefore, there can be no sorrow. Life beats at its own rhythm and at every moment it knows exactly what it wants or needs.*

It is late afternoon and we are watching a slideshow of pictures taken by Bubu. They are too many to hold my attention since I'm not a camera buff but Kovalam photos have come out nice. As twilight falls, the fireworks "bombardment" erupts from a nearby temple dedicated to a goddess. Ever since we arrived here, every evening hundreds of rounds of firecrackers are burst outside this shrine, creating a tremendous racket for miles around. These "bomb blasts" go off rapid fire with a deafening roar and billows of thick white smoke can be seen from far away. The thunderous, ear-splitting explosions are enough to wake up the dead as we feel our high-rise shudder and shake from the impact. If this continues unchecked, buildings in the temple's vicinity may develop cracks or suffer other serious damage. Manoj jokingly points to Kamal and says Capt Kamaal (Kamal means a lotus but kamaal means an extraordinary feat) should take the matter in his hands and stop this ruckus once and for all.

March 7, 2015

Today seems to be earmarked for calling on gods, goddesses and godlets. After brunch, we hopped into two cars with three temples on our list. The first two neighborhood ones, one dedicated to a local Bhagawathy (goddess) and the other to Murugan, son of

Lord Shiva who is widely worshipped in south India, turned out to be damp squibs as they were closed. We then started for the famous Chottanikkara Bhagawathy Temple. It is only about twenty kilometers away but given the poor road conditions, it promises to be a long drive. The highlight of this temple is that the goddess is believed to be an incarnation of all three principal goddesses of Hinduism. Thus, the deity is worshipped as Saraswati (learning), in the morning, as Lakshmi (wealth and prosperity) at noon and as Durga (feminine power) in the evening.

An interesting myth behind this ancient temple is that this omnipotent goddess has the power to cure people suffering from mental illnesses. In that belief, "maddies" have been brought in front of this three-in-one divinity since ages. Guha, of course, is rolling in laughter and rattling off names of friends who could benefit by coming here. However, the door to this temple is closed as well. Sigh! I feel a little let down since I was really looking forward to having a viewing of this acclaimed devi. Guha, seeing the look of disappointment on my face, said in a loud voice that I was more important than any goddess, adding, "You are living, throbbing, pulsating with life whereas she is only a figment of somebody's fertile imagination." He was right, of course, and I nodded my head in acquiescence. Since childhood I have been taught to worship and pray to the multitudinous godheads from the Hindu pantheon and it never occurred to me till I read U.G. and Guha that by doing so, I am denying the very power, the life-abiding energy residing in me and in each one of us. Isn't that sacrilegious? But as they say, old habits die hard.

It is nighttime and back in my room I am recollecting my one-on-one conversation with Guha in New York a few months ago. Here is a summary:

Dec. 12, 2014

(Ansonia, NYC)

Guha: You don't want to be here. If you had anything better to do, you wouldn't be here.

You don't have to know the goal. There is an organic necessity; it is not the goal. It's like a woman needs to get pregnant to give continuity to life – it is an organic necessity. It is doing its job. As a little girl or a boy every cell in your body knows what it needs to keep growing...

What is the struggle inside? The society, culture taught us what our aspirations should be. We have no choice but to address social needs. And we have been endowed with talents or capabilities to address these needs.

The beginning of the solution is recognizing deeply what the problem is. It is my demand and I'm not sure if that demand is aligning with my needs. In fact, the problems are real, but the solutions are fictitious, and they never work. Your head can never give solutions. The problem remains because the identification of the problem is wrong. What is my basic/root problem? The answer is creating an apparent identity. It is a continuity which is not approved by the order of the system.

If you think that the identity of Nandini is the only problem – it will shutter you. Because there IS NO NANDINI at all! There IS NO NANDINI! It is so absurd for you to accept that. What you feel, your demands, everything – they are fictitious.

~

Chapter Six

Tiger Is Out

That aloneness, when all the afflictions or desires which make the mind move are absolved, touches everything and the physical system becomes one with life. The source of our desires is the social dynamics and you are a part of the push and pull and the struggle continues. In this condition where these movements are absent, there is no spontaneous generation of desires of any kind. Even before a movement arises in the mind it absolves itself in the brain. That is kaivalya.

– Guha

March 7, 2015
Cochin

- *You torture yourself for a future that does not exist. You get the blues if you don't get an assurance of a perfect future.*
- *Our model of perfection has nothing to do with the way life is functioning.*
- *If you don't like misery, the solution is already there. But if you begin to enjoy the misery then nobody can help. Rejection is the solution.*
- *The fact that you can reason your sadness is an intellectual endeavor. The moment you are with yourself, evaluation goes on.*

- *If you cannot translate a feeling, it is never a problem. It is through translation that you create a long-term memory space. And that is derived material. It comes and goes.*
- *What you see comes and goes. Part of what you see is through very different processes and creates a long-term memory. That is the source of illusion - which you see is not there in front of you. It's a different world, it's a different beast that is in operation which recollects and recreates a parallel world.*
- *It is very difficult to maintain any relationship with someone who does not want anything from you.*

Guha has been shouting from the rooftop that the future does not exist except in my head. Now is all there is. That the parallel world we create is the problem. I translate that as peace or happiness is freedom from imaginary hopes and psychological fears. But these are all tall words and completely futile because they are not operating in me. I am always making myself miserable with expectations of a happy future or a perfect relationship. As a result, living in the moment, without any resistance on my part, is a chimera, a pipedream.

This morning, Guha is caroling his cherished Tagore songs. Rabindra Sangeet, pronounced Robindro shonggit in Bengali, comprises of songs written by Bengal's foremost poet and Nobel laureate Rabindranath Tagore. The highly distinctive and powerfully emotive compositions, numbering in thousands, have been the warp and woof of Bengali culture for over a century. I like to hear Guha sing and elucidate on Tagore's more abstract works such as on the Almighty, Creator, Universe, Truth et al. I was not disappointed as he commenced the session with *hayee akashe amar mukti* which means my emancipation is written in the skies. How beautiful. Listening to his soulful rendering stirred up deep emotions in me and when he started on *mahabiswe, mahakashe, mahakalo,* another of my favorites, I closed my eyes and let its esoteric profundity wash over me. Incidentally, he had recited the same at U.G.'s first death anniversary meeting in Bangalore in 2008. It goes:

Mahabiswe mahakashe mahakalo majhe
Aami manabo ekakee bhrami biswaye, bhrami biswaye
Tumi aachho, biswanath, aseem rahasyamaajhe
Neerabe ekakee aapan mahimaniloye
Ananta e deshkaler, aganyo e deepta loke,
Tumi aachho more chahi aami chahi toma pane
Stabdho sarbo kolahal, shantimagno charachar
Ek tumi, toma majhe aami eka nirbhoye

Amidst this vast cosmos
Encompassed by Great Time
I, a mere mortal, gasp in awe and wonder.
Thou art the Lord of the Universe,
Cloaked in unfathomable mystery
Thou do exist eternally in Your abode of glory.

In the infinity of space-time,
Through the numerous constellations
That bejewel dark space,
Thy gaze falls on me,
I gaze back at Thee.
Silence descends on this universe,
Entire creation rests in peace.
Thou Alone doeth exist and I do exist
In and through You
Thou in me.... I in Thee
Alone I dwell, ever fearless.

The line, *Tumi aachho more chahi aami chahi toma pane* is going on like a broken record in my head and while trying to find its exact meaning, I got three differing explanations:

Thy gaze falls on me, I gaze back at Thee

You look at me... And I look at You!!

Today, you look for me and I long for you

Not satisfied, I turned to Guha for help and his interpretation immediately struck a chord –*YOU are there for me, so I keep my eyes fixed on YOU.* Late at night, still chewing on that, I sat up with a jolt when it flashed that Guha's words were trying to impart an important clue. It was as if they were nudging me to wake up and pay heed to what he has been putting a heavy emphasis on, lately - remain focused and embrace the natural order of things, i.e. the vicissitudes of life. Otherwise, I will continue to be conflicted, unhappy and resistant to change. I had already received a drubbing on the subject before we embarked on our India trip.

You have so many issues, therefore very resistant to the Natural Order! You have to focus on something that you really resonate with (keep my eyes fixed on YOU or THAT?).

Only in that way other issues will drop away....

You must sort out your wants! You have to allow the energy to flow, you are very resistant!

Only focus on one suitable object that can take care of eliminating other issues!

The wandering mind wants to satisfy its agenda; they (your wants) are conflicting.

(You are) heavily conditioned. You have to reflect on this.

"It's your choice! If you want one thing it's easy. If nothing satisfies you, you can talk about THAT, until then nope!"

He was not done yet. Jabbing a finger in his chest, he blasted, "I can feel your resistance right here!" I didn't see that coming but what kind of resistance was he referring to? Could he read me like an open book? Perhaps he wanted to convey that my conditioning, my complexities, my functional reality, whatever one may call it, was preventing me from having a wholesome, harmonious synergistic interaction with the cosmos. Yes, that must be it. Now that I understood what he was driving at, I thanked him profusely and was gratified with his response, “I want my friend to be strong and vital, I want her to be a fire brand!” Again, when I acknowledged that he had nothing but my well-being at heart, I was floored when he declared, “YES, and for that I will do absolutely anything, even if you don’t approve.” It is surely a boon that Guha makes it supremely easy for us to connect with him at a very fundamental level. My interactions with him, intense at times, have not only forced me to think purposively about my life-world but also pushed me into becoming a stronger, more resilient and an independent person.

K seems to be of similar opinion as Guha, saying he had observed a different kind of “resistance” in me. He said when things did not go my way, as it often happens in life, I tended to become sullen and withdrawn, like a crab that hides between rocks. That mental egress, K cautioned, was blocking out everything, even the good things, and rebuffing good people, even my well-wishers. He implored me to be more open-minded and not obstruct the flow of life as it was harming me ultimately. Looking into my eyes, he said gently, “As your best friend, I don’t want to see you suffer anymore, so I have to tell you things straight. Awareness can help bring about change in attitude.”

Turning my attention to Guha’s outburst that I must sift through my wants and focus on just one thing, I must confess I am clueless as to what I really want. Earlier, I would have said without any hesitation “enlightenment” and nothing else but since UGG (U.G. and Guha) wiped out that concept for good from my system, I am in limbo, a void. Now what? Neither do I have even a teeny-weeny bit of interest left in any kind of reading material, including spiritual or philosophical, nor do I care to indulge in conventional social customs and interactions. Then what should I do with my time? “Write,” he replied. “You have vast life experience which you can integrate with your current journaling.” Viola! Thus, was born the idea of taking up this Guha-centric work. It is a huge blessing because it has turned out to be the best therapy to heal and let go of past hurts.

In hindsight, it was at Radhika's house where the main shock of Guha's "resistance" movement took place. On a wintry weekend, after a traditional south Indian meal we were sitting around relaxed, discussing this, that or the other when the rumblings began. Guha, in front of everyone, began to provoke me by joking about my vulnerabilities and asking very personal, uncomfortable questions about my relationships, life choices, failures, etc. Totally unprepared and mortified at such an onslaught in a public setting, I began to quake in fear and trepidation. Guha was relentless and kept up the pressure even though I was fumbling, and my replies were getting more and more incoherent with every passing minute. I was making a big fool of myself, no doubt, and hated Guha for putting me through this ordeal. As I felt the ground slipping away under my feet, I remembered Sita in *Ramayana* and wished mother earth would swallow me up and save me from this humiliation. Everyone was watching in pin-drop silence and dare not interrupt. But as everything in life has a beginning and an end, the temblor too came to pass, and I ran out, wiping away tears of anger and frustration. From now on, I will never divulge anything to Guha ever again, I vowed to myself.

What happened there, really? What was Guha trying to achieve? Perhaps he was experimenting with his "perturbation theory" in an effort to break the ego "I"'s stranglehold on the system. That's it! That was his aim right from the start, I realized in a daze. Alas, the wily "I", sensing danger to its authority, managed to slither away and hide in the vast labyrinth of the mind. A great opportunity was lost as the interloper prevailed, stronger than ever. At the very least, this whole exercise taught me a lesson to never again doubt Guha's intentions. The real enemy was within, not Guha, who will always remain a true friend to the bitter end.

Coming back to "keep my eye fixed on you", the phrase reminds me of an incident that Guha has narrated to us on many occasions and which he has dwelt upon at length in *14 Days in Palm Springs with U.G.*: Once U.G. and Guha were taking a stroll outside the Ocotillo

Lodge when Guha casually remarked that many considered H. W. L. Poonja aka Papaji, a well-known guru, to be the spiritual heir to Ramana Maharshi. Poonja was still alive when this episode took place in 1995. During Ramana's lifetime, Poonja visited the sage a number of times whom he revered as his master. But Ramana never recognized any relationship with anybody, let alone a guru-disciple one. Perhaps to some, Poonja's long association with Ramana implied a kind of endorsement they sought about his "liberation" and eligibility to be deemed as Ramana's successor. Coming back to our story, when U.G. heard this, he stopped abruptly in his tracks, turned to face Guha and said in a grave tone, "Look into my eyes and repeat what you just said." Guha literally froze, his head spinning, trying to digest what U.G. was alluding to. Now, as I ponder about this supercharged exchange, was U.G. implying that if anyone, it was him who was Ramana's torch-bearer? I have not read anywhere that U.G. ever admitted anything to that effect. On the contrary, he denounced gurus and was wont to say, *a true guru will tell you to stand on your own two feet, to throw away all the crutches. You can walk and if you fall, you will rise and walk again.* Twice I asked Guha if U.G. and he both debunked the concept of a guru in the traditional sense. No reply. For argument's sake, if I were to believe in guru-disciple lineage, where would that leave me? A staunch devotee of Ramana for many years, I was pulled by U.G.'s philosophy (fatal attraction, Guha never tires of telling me), and ended up with Guha, one of U.G.'s closest friends. Holy moly!

March 8, 2015

Ambuja, senior executive with a large bank, arrived from Hyderabad last night. Despite her busy schedule she managed to take time off for a quick visit before Guha left Cochin. This morning, she is eagerly inviting Guha to be the first guest at her soon-to-be-ready vacation home in Mysore. Lucky Ambuja, for she is retiring in summer. Having read U.G. extensively, she is curious to learn more about Guha's relationship with him. Guha begins with:

Superconducting proximity effect: *Superconductivity is a special state of matter where there is no resistance at all. This is an exotic state which can be induced in a material close to the superconductor. I (Guha) was completely perplexed at the way things were turning in my body. I, of course, didn't know what was going on in U.G.'s body. At that time, I used to feel very high, very healthy and extremely energetic and wanted to push everybody to U.G. I started thinking what could it be? The model is created by mind. Life's principle cannot be generalized; it is not physics. U.G. used to say, 'I like the fact that you are working on superconductivity. Life though doesn't always work that way.' No example can ever be given that mimics the dynamic equilibrium of life. For me, no water could extinguish the fire within me.*

Algae effect: *Sometimes life cracks open the coverings to give us a glimpse of its power and existence. When you throw a stone in a lake filled with algae, it gives you a glimpse of the clear water underneath but is soon covered up again.*

I can totally relate to Guha that he felt euphoric in U.G.'s company. Sometime ago, Guha along with Julie and Louis Brawley, a close friend of U.G. and the Guha family, came to meet me in Princeton. We were sitting in a tea room with Louis regaling us with YouTube videos on his phone which U.G. was fond of watching, the themes being money is all, love doesn't exist. Listening to Louis' hysterical comments alongside the songs, I was doubled up with laughter, so much so that my stomach muscles were hurting and streams of tears were pouring out of my eyes. That was the beginning of the madness which continued for the rest of the day. After taking their leave, I still could not contain myself and dissolved into uncontrollable laughter just looking at passersby. While driving to a friend's place blurry-eyed and laughing like a lunatic, I noticed an old lady shaking her head and rolling her eyes at me in disgust. Can't blame her if she assumed I was high on weed. Even when I was talking to my pal I had to exercise superhuman will power not to burst out giggling. Once home, my son kept giving me looks of amused puzzlement as he saw me cracking up without any rhyme or reason. That got me going even more and I had to bolt to the patio several times to laugh out loud. The insanity continued till I went to bed chuckling and chortling. Guha explained later, endorphins, the feel-good neurochemicals, can get activated or released when the system is totally relaxed. "Can it be due to the superconducting proximity effect," I questioned. His answer: "Sure, it depends. If you feel good and unencumbered in someone's company, you will laugh more. Doctors say laughter is the best medicine and has more beneficial effects than being sad."

Our second last day in Cochin, which had started on a calm note, got wackier and wackier as hours ticked by. Mid-morning Guha announced we would eat lunch at the nearby five-star Crowne Plaza Hotel where they serve a grand buffet albeit an expensive one. That was when the drama began as Manoj started pestering me to foot the bill for the entire group. Earlier, I had already discussed this with Guha and he had hesitantly acquiesced that I could treat us all, if I wished. Perhaps Manoj was unhappy that I may be getting a free ride from Guha, so took it upon himself to extract dues from me somehow. He may not have realized yet that no one can stay even for a minute with Guha without his nod, money or not. A little upset, I took his jibes in my stride consoling myself that I was here as Guha's guest and need not concern myself with anyone else's agenda.

As luck would have it, I found Manoj sitting right opposite at the lunch table and he made the most of this opportunity to needle me throughout the meal. In the bargain, I did not relish any of the delicious dishes in front of me. Manoj's wife Vidya, who was seated next to him, tried her best to persuade him to drop the subject, but like a vulture after its prey, he kept coming after me. Unfortunately, I too went on the offensive arguing back vociferously, but that fired him up even more. Everyone was observing the duel with amusement and Guha did not interfere even once. Ambuja, however, sensing I was majorly piqued, tried her best to pacify me, appealing not to retort back. But would I listen? The bitter sparring continued till Manoj followed Guha and others to the veranda after they were done eating. With Ambuja, Vidya and I left behind I quickly summoned the waiter for the bill, impatient to get away. Despite my plea, our man took his time and when he did show up, he did not have the check with him. Someone had already made the payment, he announced. After all the shenanigans, this was not only an anticlimax, but a huge surprise too. Upon enquiry, it transpired that Sanjiv was the big-hearted hero. Full of thankfulness, I asked him the reason behind his magnanimity and found his matter-of-fact reply very touching, "Why should you pay, you don't even have a job."

Back home I shut myself in my room, emotionally worn out with hot tears running down my cheeks. In Guha's presence, even the littlest of things get amplified. After a short nap, I felt restored and revived, determined more than ever to fight fire with fire. I refused to be intimidated or be trampled upon by anyone ever again. Throughout the evening, we were predictably at each other's throats, squabbling over silly things. By the time we were ready to retire for the night, Manoj's comebacks were sounding feeble and he seemed to be running out of steam. Conversely, I was energized, ready to take up cudgels till kingdom come. For everyone else, this was good entertainment. The ego "I" can go to any length, even indulging in such petty pastimes to protect its identity, I was learning.

Incidentally, Manoj was a U.G. "goner" for a long time, but after meeting Guha, he has now become a Guha "goner". I admire his intensity and one-pointedness towards Guha although he tends to get carried away by his own enthusiasm. In his excitement, he keeps interrupting Guha while the latter is talking, even shouting over him to get his point across. This may sound funny, but it can be very disruptive.

March 9, 2015

The D-day has finally arrived. The Cochin camp is disbanding, and soon we will part ways. Most are traveling with Guha to Delhi where he will be in transit for a short time. The entourage will then proceed to a place called Parwanoo, located in the sub-Himalayan Shiwalik mountain range, on the highway to Shimla. Sanjay, the lawyer, who owns a place there, invited Guha to spend a few days with him. I am flying to Mumbai to meet my family and will catch up with Guha later. He has promised to receive K and I at Chandigarh airport and accompany us to Parwanoo, a drive of about 21 miles. I am sad that my stay with Guha has come to an end. Living in such close quarters with him and Julie was a privilege and who knows when I will get such a chance again.

Ambuja is here bright and early, listening closely to Guha:

When you are struggling you still want to know why. The questioner is never exhausted. The mechanism itself cannot do anything to itself to stop this questioning. Anything you want is food for that engine. Your existence knows what it needs to maintain its equilibrium. Any movement that gives you additional information is fuel for that movement.

Kishor, Manoj and Sanjiv tiptoe in. Sanjiv is quiet and speaks only when necessary. He is very much affected by Guha and always listens to him with full attention, most of the time with eyes closed. Occasionally, he seems to be in a trance or lost in meditation, appearing like the Buddha. At other times, he looks visibly shaken, tears streaming down his face. The talk continues....

When the push comes, you will go down on your knees and look for a savior. The movement didn't do its job. The questioner didn't end.

Life is complete by itself at the onset. It's not a matter of understanding.

If your near and dear ones are sick, no one will touch them if you don't have money.

– Bye, bye Cochin.

March 20, 2015
New Jersey

The last leg of our India trip was delightfully eventful. After arriving in Parwanoo, we had a sumptuous lunch of north Indian curries and breads on a terrace restaurant overlooking the valley and the hills. Thereafter, we immediately started up the mountain road to Kasauli, which is halfway to Shimla, capital of Himachal Pradesh. Shimla is nestled amidst snow-clad peaks at an altitude of over 7000 feet and sounds very inviting, but we do not have time to visit the scenic town on this trip.

Not too far from Kasauli, we decided to halt at the well-known Manki Point/Sanjeevani Hanuman Temple. There is an interesting legend from *Ramayana* behind this temple located on top of the foot-shaped hill. When monkey-god Hanuman was returning from the Himalayas after procuring the magical, life-giving Sanjeevani herb, one of his feet touched the hill which is why it resembles a foot. He had embarked on the voyage at the behest of Lord Rama whose brother Lakshmana was on his deathbed from battle wounds and could only be revived by this divine herb. The name Manki Point was given in honor of the priest by that name who built the hilltop temple. That entire area falls under military jurisdiction and access to this restricted zone is controlled by the Indian Air Force. Once inside, we walked about half a mile to reach the foot of the hill and from there onwards we had to climb hundreds of uneven steps to reach the top. The ascent was steep but not overly strenuous and with ample resting points along the way we reached the shrine in about half hour without much trouble.

After paying my respects to one of the most celebrated gods in India, I came out in the open for some fresh air. Here I was taken aback to see a small helipad which I learnt was for military purposes only. From the vantage point, I admired the surrounding mountain ranges and the Shimla valley with the Sutlej river winding through the plains like a silvery thread. Yonder, I could see Chandigarh glittering under the bright sunlight. The quiet, peaceful ambiance coupled with the cool breeze fanning my face was not only soothing but infused me with new energy. Mission completed, we quickly sprinted down to rejoin Guha and others who did not accompany us on the pilgrimage.

On the road again, we stopped at a small wayside tea shop for our evening cupper. "G-Force" was at its most intense and Manoj-Nandini bantering was going full throttle. And Guha being Guha, kept adding fuel to the fire. According to him, Manoj and I are like siblings, always competing for attention. He says Manoj brings out a very different aspect of my personality, fiery and full of energy, sort of like a tigress looking for a fresh kill. So, while the tea was brewing, a full-fledged argument was simmering between Manoj and myself, who knows about what. As we locked horns, everyone was enjoying the merry spectacle. The fight continued unabated with neither party willing to concede defeat, but I was fast reaching the end of my tether. But Guha would not allow me to give up, "Come on, after a visit to the Hanuman temple you should be energized. Fire back!" After all, Hanuman is the god of strength and courage. With that rallying cry, the entire gang started chanting the unrivaled *Hanuman Chalisa*[5] on top of their voices with tremendous gusto, accompanied by vigorous clapping and loud clanging of spoons. And Guha just sat there beaming and brimming with laughter. Needless to say, Guha and his brigade, not Hanuman, revived the flagging spirits of this damsel in distress and the enemy was vanquished effortlessly. Oh, what a rollicking time we had! Julie, of course, recorded the entire proceedings.

I must recount another hilarious incident, this one also involving dear Manoj. The momentous holiday coming to an end, our cavalcade was on its way to New Delhi airport. We were spread out in three cars – Manoj, Vidya, their son and Guha in Manoj's car with Vidya at the wheel, Julie, Kamal and I following them at a distance in a taxi and the rest in Sanjay's SUV. As we were nearing our destination, we lost track of Guha's car and even when we reached the airport, there was no sign

---

5 *A devotional hymn of forty verses in praise of the deity*

of them. A little concerned, Kamal phoned Guha to ascertain their whereabouts. They had fallen far behind and were still thirty minutes away. Guha said the car was making weird noises and was keeping his fingers crossed that it would not break down. Anyway, we kept waiting to hear back from Guha but after another half an hour there was again no word from him. Anxious, Kamal called Guha once more. As he was talking to him, I heard him go, "Oh no, omg, is everyone okay" followed by peals of his full-throated laughter. I heaved a sigh of relief. I would soon know the full story, but it sounded like there was no serious mishap.

Here's what befell the hapless passengers. The minute Guha said he hoped the car would not give any trouble Manoj's rickety ol' jalopy shook, shuddered and stopped dead in the middle of the busy roadway. I could visualize them standing dejected on the side of the road in the sweltering mid-day Delhi heat. As Guha was frantically looking for a cab, Manoj was shouting into his cell phone trying to get hold of a tow truck service. It turned out to be a long wait before one showed up. Luckily for Guha, he managed to get an auto rickshaw and with luggage on his knees, reached the airport in the nick of time for his flight. I later learnt that Manoj had proposed the idea of going on a road trip with Guha from New Delhi to Cochin, a distance of about 1700 miles, in that tin lizzie! What was he thinking?

~

Chapter Seven

Thoughts Drain Energy

The so-called choice we think we have is not a choice at all. Our conditioning is sorting information inside us and throwing out subjective interpretations of that information.

– Guha

March 30, 2015
New Jersey

The Hindus from early days were always searching for "permanence". They were trying to distinguish between ephemeral and eternal, i e Anitya and Nitya in this phenomenal world. They believed that human suffering was caused by not realizing "the Truth that is unchanging". To be free from this suffering, from the bondage of illusion or what they termed "unreal", they came up with the concept of mukti, moksha, or emancipation, which would follow by realizing the Truth that is real. This abstraction they termed Brahman. Thus, Brahman was a logically ascertained premise. They then went on to search for the unchangeable Truth in this world of constant change and developed the process of "neti, neti," which means negation of anything and everything that changes.

While trying to discover such a condition or state, they came to an absolute "give up" point. The "give up" is when one discovers that the mental movement which wants to figure out something that is real, finds – to its absolute and utter dismay – that it cannot do a damn thing about illusion; it is the mental movement that creates the unreal! However, if the "give-up" can sustain itself, eventually it may break the continuity of thought. And if that happens, it can change the entire chemistry of the body and create an enormous high that no alcohol or drug can match. That high becomes an object of reality and is described in the scriptures as "continuous or permanent bliss". But such descriptions create a myth, a story, which is misleading. The main point to note is there is no guarantee that this "give up" will produce such a state, and as such the scriptures refer to this as: "to whomsoever it chooses ... "

– Guha

When I stumbled upon this buried treasure, what was immediately striking was Guha's originality of thought and penetrating insights into age-old concepts about Reality and Brahman. Guha the scientist's concise and rational analysis of such a complex subject matter literally took my breath away. I remember reading Guha's talks on the web before I met him. At that time, I was a model aspirant who was assiduously following the motto I had assigned to myself – simple living, high thinking and a life dedicated to spiritual matters. Thus, piety, humility, goodness was to be adorned like ornaments while continuously practicing self-enquiry like a monk. So naturally, Guha's words made no sense at all. But like a moth drawn to a flame, I kept coming back again and again, without understanding why. One day, I resolved to meet Guha personally and get everything sorted out for my peace of mind. That meeting was a watershed moment, a point of no return. Old theories and notions were duly cast off, just as a snake sheds its skin at the right time to allow for further growth. To follow something written in a book long time ago was not acceptable anymore as a major internal reshuffle demanded corresponding validity from the system and a careful examination of my belief structure. Now every thought that arises is up for scrutiny, only to be discarded as my conditioning, my samskaras, my genetic make-up, not me, not me. Maybe this is what is meant by conducting my own self-enquiry to find out for myself who am I? Perhaps this is what the seers of yore termed "neti, neti", the process of negation.

Back home in New Jersey I am still trying to get back into routine after a frenetic, chaotic but an unforgettable Indian odyssey with Guha. What a paradox my erstwhile motherland is. On the one hand, the hospitality, the vibrancy, the throbbing, pulsating energy of this colorful nation is truly amazing. On the other, the filth, heat, dust pollution, noise, traffic, not to forget the throngs of people everywhere, can make you go nuts. Being with Guha, though, you don't much care what's happening around you, things seem to fall in place of their own accord. Car is at your doorstep when you want to move, food appears when you are hungry, and shelter has already been taken care of wherever you happen to be. If nothing works out, he will offer you his couch. It is simple when you have just one focus, Guha has told me a million times.

Despite the jetlag, here I am at Julie's early in the morning to spend the entire day with Guha. We are waiting for Shujaat, a child psychiatrist and a good friend of his, to arrive from upstate New York. A seeker since he was a young boy, his rarefied quest came to a grinding halt after he met Guha through my acquaintance. While growing up in Pakistan he was inadvertently drawn to Sufism, the esoteric dimension of Islam and yearned to be like the mystics who sang and preached divine love. In the bargain, he got passionate about devotional Sufi music inspired by works of Rumi, Bulleh Shah, Amir Khusrow and Hafiz. After migrating to USA, Shujaat became well-versed with mainstream Hindu thought and sought out many so-called enlightened masters. Finally, he came across Ramana and began to practice his philosophy in right earnest. Later, he became a follower of V. Ganesan, grandnephew of Ramana Maharshi and their close association lasted for a decade till Guha came into the picture.

I was introduced to Shujaat when he and Ganesanji visited me for a brief stay. Earlier, when I was on a sojourn to Ramanasram in Tiruvannamalai, I had made it a point to meet Ganesanji and extend to him an open invitation to look me up when he next came to US. I respected him for his devoutness, his espousal of spiritual values, as well as his lifelong, unswerving service to Ramana devotees and other saints. Moreover, the thought that he was Ramana's blood relative was very strong in me and felt my life mission would be accomplished to host such a personage. Therefore, I was delighted when he took up my offer to put up at my place and give a series of talks in New Jersey. However, by the time he arrived at my doorstep a few months later, the tide had already turned. The UGG cyclone had struck but I stood by my commitment to host Ganesanji.

During their visit, the preceptor and his companion would rise early and discuss metaphysical matters in hushed tones over their first cupper. With no more burning questions, I took my time to join them. One morning, when I came downstairs, there was no sound and no sign of my guests. A little bewildered, I went looking for them and found Ganesanji in the living room sitting alone with eyes closed in front of Ramana's portrait. I waited till he came out of his meditation to enquire about Shujaat's absence. He replied that he had not seen Shujaat at all since he woke up which confounded me even more. Full of remorse that I was not up earlier to cater to his needs, I quickly made Ganesanji tea and breakfast. About an hour later, Shujaat walked in looking haggard and sleep-deprived. He apologized for his late arrival saying he had a bad migraine and could not get a wink of sleep. Later, when Ganesanji was taking a nap in the afternoon, Shujaat and I got talking and that was when he confided that he frequently suffered from acute headaches and bodyaches. Sometimes, the pain was so severe that he was not able to perform even the simplest of daily tasks. Also, he had lost all drive to work, he only wanted *mukti*, nothing more, nothing less. I then informed him about Guha, his close friendship with U.G. and the physical changes and pain he had undergone before coming into the Natural State. Perhaps it would be beneficial for Shujaat to meet Guha who may be able to shed some light on the cause of his suffering. Well, Guha's name fell on receptive ears, a meeting was arranged and the rest, as they say, is history!

Lunch over, I helped Julie with the dishes and afterwards we got engrossed in a film on the Church of Scientology on CNN. While we were watching, Radhika walked in. Fortunately, she works close by and takes every available opportunity to leave early to spend time with Guha. After a while, I casually remarked that Hinduism as a religion had some good points. Hearing that, Guha got alarmingly animated; looked like I had stirred a hornet's nest. "Your religion is horrible," he shouted, hands flailing, almost jumping out of his seat with rage. "It allows mothers and sisters to be killed in the name of religion. They tell women to treat their husbands (pati) like parmeswar (god), then they shove the widows on to the funeral pyre along with their dead husbands!" He was referring to the former Hindu practice of Sati, outlawed since long, of a widow being forced to immolate herself on her dead husband's funeral pyre. He continued to talk fiercely about the woes of Hinduism, berating Vedic seers for misleading humanity: "Those guys created a fictitious reality – drinking soma juice, smoking hashish and talking about love, bliss, beatitude. They made us believe that striving for these things should be the meaning and purpose of our life."

On to other things:

- *Understand! The movement that is created for seeking external harmony is false. The human idea disturbs the equilibrium. Ideas always want something which is not what the system needs. Don't do anything. Leave it alone.*
- *Feel whatever you want to feel, don't impose it on others. Don't turn it into a sales pitch.*
- *You can't accept "just as is" out there. You have to exemplify because you can think.*

- *When you realize how much part of what you think has gone to create struggle, destroy life and properties, you'll be surprised.*
- *They took everything from the American Indians and in return gave them small pox blankets! You don't feel a damn thing for anybody. You are shedding crocodile tears!*
- *Money is related to power. Why do you look up to Bill Gates? It is because he can make a huge difference in people's lives. Life means, what they think is living. In earlier times in India, someone who had Rs 1 crore (about $135000) used to be looked upon as Koteshwar or god of ten million. They were considered equivalent to god because they had the power to change the lives of scores of people.*

Suddenly, turning to Radhika, he demanded: "Why do you want to listen to me at all?"

Radhika: "Let me figure it out and then I'll let you know why I listen to you. I have waited over 50 years to find you. I'm not going in search of someone else at this stage."

Feeling quite happy for some reason, I was smiling incessantly. "Endorphin release," Guha said. "They are shiny little happy molecules," he added laughingly.

April 2, 2015

Guha narrated a funny but a stirring exchange between U.G. and himself:

G: U.G., I have bought a ticket for India. I would like to go in October and see my mother.

U.G: Oh, why do you want to go India? It's a spiritual shitland! And in October? That's not your vacation time.

G: I have to visit my mother. She desperately wants to see me. I haven't seen her in six years and she is not keeping well.

U.G: Oh, she has done her job, bringing a horrible person like you in this world! Let her go. Old people should die.

G: But U.G., I have to go. I have already bought the ticket.

U.G: How much did you spend on the ticket?

G: $1500

U.G: Okay, you do one thing. Instead of going to India, buy a ticket to Switzerland and come here and see me instead. I will give you the money for your India ticket.

G: Okay

U.G: By the way, I heard you got some bonus? How much did you get?

G: How did you know? I got $5000.

As it turned out, Guha purchased a ticket to Switzerland, gave his entire bonus to U.G. and never got the promised funds for the India ticket. He did not question U.G. even once and followed his every word to the letter. So deep was his love for U.G. Luckily, Guha was able to travel to India at a later date and meet his mother just before she took her last breath.

April 4, 2015

Guha, Shujaat, Radhika and I are busy making small talk while having our afternoon tea/coffee at Julie's. It is spring time, and love is in the air! Guha, looking amused, wants to know why everyone is in the mood to exchange love songs. He is referring to a romantic song that Revathi just sent. She lives far away and longs to be with Guha, the love of her life. Thus, one of the ways to alleviate her separation pangs is to keep bombarding the object of her affection with electronic love missives. If his phone is turned off, she doesn't give up, she sends them via Julie. Guha promptly forwarded her latest communique to Shujaat. That was a big no, no as it is no secret that Shujaat is a diehard skeptic about matters of the heart. Cupid is stupid, he declares. A testy exchange ensued on love and broken hearts between Revathi and Shujaat which Julie read aloud:

Shujaat: "… I've been through that *mast* (crazy) love a few times. It's an intoxicating high … just neurotransmitter and hormone-based delusional game." Quoting Tina Turner, he added, "Love is a second-hand emotion. Who needs a heart when a heart can be broken?"

Revathi's spirited rejoinder: "So, I guess this is how guys bromance. Very different and clinical compared to women. Ha! Ha! Glad to know my texts are being evaluated by a psychiatrist. Feel I'm truly blessed and in safe hands. Any guy or gal who is willing to sing the song to Guha that Shujaat did (Bulleh Shah's *Pehle pagal karte ho, phir deewana kehte ho* – first you make me mad after you, then you call me a romantic) can never insulate himself from love or a broken heart. Neurotransmitters or hormones be damned."

Radhika chimed in: "Her wit has improved ten-fold." Julie's swift response, "Okay, but no more of those jokes, please." She was now referring to R & R's penchant for sharing jokes from *desi* WhatsApp group forums to Guha who would read those aloud to us. Julie can't stand these, and neither can I. In my opinion, they highlight male chauvinism at its worst and clearly showcase the hypocritical and belittling mindset that many men have towards women. The tigress in me is coming out. Grrr!

Guha gets serious:

- *The sense of self is built to satisfy your desires. Your intentions are built by struggles from childhood. Anything you do is the intention of thought.*
- *There's so much additional living energy inside the body when it is not stressed by your anxieties, worries and goal-oriented activities…. Your thoughts are draining life's energy. It's the body's struggle – it wants to maintain equilibrium at all times, but the sense of self is obstructing it. The body is trying to break down the experiencing structure to live better.*
- *How can you own another human being? Is it even possible? We can*

be so myopic. We shudder at the thought if anyone wants to own us.

- *The intelligence through which the system works, it reaches so far it is mind boggling. The system knows how to take care of itself. If a woman is pregnant, she gets an enormous amount of protection from Nature. That's the design of life. That knowledge is more encompassing than anything you plan.*
- *My father who was a doctor used to say that the patient thinks the doctor is god but actually he knew nothing is in our hands.*
- *Vibhuti is the magical power of life. The most mysterious and magical is your relationship with yourself.*
- *Life is a series of uncontrollable incidents. Know the unknowability of the source movement of life. The source movement is always hidden. Unless you project a future that is conducive to your goals you cannot live peacefully in the present. The movement of thought needs to create that knowable future. However, thoughts of engineering that knowable future are destroying the peace in the present.*
- *There is no such thing as achieving something beyond mind. By inventing something that is beyond mind, the mind assures of its dominance and its continuity on the system. Otherwise, it is a false proposition to start with. How can you ever reach the unknown? Reaching implies known. Perhaps you will be there one day – hope never dies, the goal never goes away.*
- *The perceptive reality is not allowing me to conjure up ideas to disturb the flow at this moment.*
- *I have no desire but that doesn't mean I am not going to participate.*

Late afternoon, we decided to go for a drive along Canal Road in Franklin town which is not too far from Julie's house. Cruising down the scenic route, peeping through the tall trees, the canal and the adjoining tow path veer in and out of our view. On the other side, there are old houses and historic homes but not that many, so it's just you, the tree-lined, narrow, winding road, open fields and the woods. How peaceful it is here. This stretch is part of the 70-mile

Delaware & Raritan Canal which is the Garden State's most popular recreational corridor for walking, jogging, bicycling, canoeing, etc. We come here frequently in warm weather for morning walks and Julie loves this area so much that she may end up buying an estate here one day. Incidentally, Franklin is consistently rated one of the top ten places to live in the US.

During the ride, we listened to yet another Bollywood number, again sent by Revathi to her dearest Guha. As soon as it was over, the conversation went something like this:

Radhika: When did we last have a session of listening to Hindi romantic songs?

I: All the way from Chicago to New Jersey. (Everyone laughs.)

I was referring to our road trip a few months ago.

Radhika: Get ready to listen to them when we drive to South Carolina.

I thought to myself, oh no, not again. I am not very fond of Bollywood songs.

I (in jest): Maybe we can fly to South Carolina instead of driving.

Guha (to me): Maybe you should not come to South Carolina.

I: Okay, I won't come if you don't want me to.

Guha (sensing I was a little vexed) added jokingly: "Then I can't leave."

Sometimes I get annoyed with myself for taking the bait so easily. Every now and then Guha likes to tease us that we need not waste our time by coming to meet him or travel with him when he knows very well that we would give an arm and a leg to do so. After all, we genuinely want to spend as much time with him as possible, no matter where he goes or who he meets. Is he testing us? Oh well, I thought to myself, if I don't go on this trip, I can hunker down and finish a big chunk of editing work for the forthcoming book on Guha's talks. After returning from our excursion, we began to review the manuscript in great detail.

April 8, 2015

Ila from Kolkata arrived yesterday. She runs a sweetshop and she is as sweet as the sweets she sells. The family-owned "Mithai", which literally means sweet, is such a well-known place and their wares so sought-after in this populous city that a public bus stop has been named after it. Ila brought us boxes of mouth-watering *sandesh* which she got made especially for us. So sweet! Pronounced *shondesh* in Bengali, this delicious milk and sugar sweetmeat is highly coveted all over India and is my best-loved sugary confection. Whenever Guha and friends are camping in Kolkata, Ila unfailingly sends them delectable treats like *rosogollas, rasa malais* or *mishti doi* in its traditional brown mud pot every single day. Yummm!

Ila lives with her husband in a lovely bungalow not too far from her store and in her spare time pursues her hobby to learn singing. Her tutor is none other than Bubu, Guha's friend, and it is through him that she came under Guha's ambit. Initially, it was Guha who pulled her out of a difficult situation and turned her life around. Now her health has improved dramatically, she is brimming with self-confidence and even travels abroad by herself to be with him. She trusts Guha implicitly and does not take any major decisions before seeking his advice. She considers and addresses him as Dada, which means elder brother, one who is only interested in your well-being. I made up the last part but that's the kind of brother he is to me too. Ila's father also had tremendous love and respect for Guha and to such a degree that he always consulted Guha regarding his family assets and properties. Intriguingly, the last time he invited Guha, he dressed head to foot in full ethnic regalia and paid obeisance to Guha as though to a guru. Shortly thereafter, he passed away peacefully.

April 15, 2015

Ansonia

Guha drove us all, Ila, Julie and I to the city as Matthew from Brooklyn is expected at lunchtime. An avid reader, he devoured J. Krishnamurti and U.G. books but got hooked to U.G. "That's the

U.G. Krishnamurti phenomenon," Guha exclaimed. He tries to meet Guha as often as he can since he genuinely enjoys discussing UGG ideology with him and Guha too likes getting down to the brass tacks with him.

A freelance videographer, Matt has been working on a documentary film on U.G. for the last seven years. He has travelled far and wide to interview not only surviving U.G. friends but interestingly, foes too. According to Guha, "U.G. caught this youngster's imagination very deeply. He wanted to do a documentary on him but not from the point of view of a devotee of a religious leader. Devotees always want to exemplify, epitomize everything about their guru but Matthew would have none of that. He was interested in making an in-depth, objective documentary based on hard facts for all audiences. So, along with interviewing U.G. fans, he also went and met people who hated U.G. with a vengeance. When I saw some of the clips, I was like oh my god! I explained to him that the main thing about these people's hatred for U.G. shows a tremendously positive aspect about him. This is what happens - you get obsessive about one thing or one person. They could not handle U.G.'s intensity, his focus, but could not dismiss him either."

Matt was exposed to an alternative lifestyle from childhood as his mother was part of a Christian sect. I have read and seen around me children who grew up in a toxic environment - where freedom of thought and authentic self-expression was denied, where the doors of questioning and curiosity were slammed, where the cult leader was worshipped like god - having serious repercussions for the rest of their lives. But I want to know from Guha if they manage to get out, are they spurred to find their own path as they grow older? Guha replies, "These are innocent, curious kids who have been told of a possibility of a promised land, a promised state, a promised freedom which never materialized for them. They were surrounded by people who were way below par, below the standards they were preaching unless they were adept at putting up a façade. So, that Promised Land is always lurking in the background. Whether they are searching or not, if they suddenly hear something, they tend to read, to figure things out. Obviously, the Promised Land is always in the imagination but at least it can shake you up very deep from the core."

Guha continues, "Growing up in such an environment can go two ways – either they become very dogmatic or extremely cynical and skeptical because in that atmosphere, the authority and irrationality are so high the children get tortured and they get 'closed'. There is nothing blooming there, it's like a forced condition. Most religious cultures are cultish. Forcing a young kid to read only scriptures or religious books and nothing else is devastating. He is like a small frog living in a small well where the water is filthy, rotten, and unusable; he can't breathe. Such a child is deprived of interactions that are real and healthy for the consciousness.... Even if by a miracle he comes out of that world, it is very hard for him to adjust in the open world, just as a person who is freed from jail after 30 years is unable to fit into a normal world. The whole organism goes into a catatonic state in a very oppressive way. They cannot regulate themselves."

~

Chapter Eight

The Natural Man

There are some life abiding feelings. There is no gap between need and want. That is the action. Thoughts are slow because they separate.
– Guha

A few months ago, I went through a brief phase of writing "poetry". When the system is totally relaxed, unburdened and unencumbered, it can release endorphins, Guha says. Perhaps it is an effect of being in Guha's company and these spontaneous, effortless outpourings are the outcome.

The first five are limericks, playful and light-hearted, next the two sonnets – the first, my life in a nutshell, the other conveying my love for Guha and the meadows near to where I live, followed by some other verses written on different occasions.

There once was a man named Guha
Who came from the land of Durga
He writhed in pain
And became Superman
He now lives in No Man's Land
I love Guha, the Natural Man

I love Guha, the Mirthful Man
Love and laughter
Joy and rapture
Makes me love Guha all over again

The system is a powerful thing, "I" a poor thing
The system is intelligent, "I" is belligerent
The system is SILENCE
The "I" is turbulence
The system is KOTU, King of the Universe

Shiva dances than, than, than
Guha roars dham, dham, dham
Fearful Rudra tandava
Cheerful Guha ananda
Make the world go round o' round

I say love you, you say forsake you
I say love you, you say leave you
Sad and sorrowful
Lost and pitiful
Walk by my side, I beseech you

The Trident

The tale of terrific trident begins at fifty
Hark! Childhood was a mess; woeful, fearful
Sad and pitiful, life seemed pretty nasty
Youth was disastrous, marriage disgraceful
Morbid and pernicious life was unbearable
Then came Agastya, harbinger of happiness
My bundle of joy made things quite bearable
Silent and sagacious, seeped with sweetness
Agastya, my beloved son, you are adorable

On a wintry day, oh so mad with bitterness
Hubby dear yells you are not at all lovable
Bang! The door slams, flower wilts with sadness
Enter mighty Guha wielding trident of love, joy, laughter
Trident sharp pierces my heart and love blossoms ever after

The Meadows

As dawn breaks we march in meadows of Mercer
In woodlands, grasslands, marshes and farmland
Peaceful and tranquil are the meadows of Mercer
On gravel paths, boardwalks, treading by the lakeside
Behold pretty wildflowers in the meadows of Mercer
Violets, daisies, buttercups, asters bright and white
Dainty little bluebells winking in meadows of Mercer
Spot here a bobolink swinging on the grassy stem
Or a teeny tiny turtle hiding in meadows of Mercer
Watch the red-winged butterfly's fluttering flight
Or the feisty kestrel flapping its tail with all might
Oh! It's a golden day in the meadows of Mercer
With Guha at my side I am brimming with delight
Marvels of Nature Guha and meadows of Mercer

Web of Love

Ask me not if I miss him
Ask me not if I long for him
Ask me not if I truly adore him
All I know is Guha has me all entangled
In a web of love, so deeply subliminal

A Million Thanks

On this Winter Solstice a few random thoughts, observations and reflections – all of my own making:

Like I recall meeting you on a cold wintry morning eons ago

Like you were perched royally on the sofa as Julie dozed by your side
Like I remember your twinkling eyes, merry laughter listening to my Ramana rant
Like I had no idea I was entering the lion's den with exits closed and no way out
Like then why do I feel unshackled, unburdened and happy like a sprite?
Like why do I think I have met my mentor, teacher, best friend, guiding light?
Like how can I repay one who wants nothing but one who gives day and night?
Like finally my clumsy words hope to convey lucky I am to have you in my life
A million thanks to you Guhaji, now and forever in time.

Thank You
Thank you, thank you, thank you
On this Thanksgiving Day I thank you
Whether near or far across the seven seas
You are always in my heart, seated so deep
Full of gratitude and praise, I fold my hands
And offer a million thanks to Natural Man

What is Reality?
Reality
Functional Reality
Reality is Subjective
Subject Specific Functional Reality
SSFR!

~

Chapter Nine

Align With Nature

We are all same in the game of life and we are all unique because the way it is formed has enormous diversity. (Similarities between species are more than dissimilarities.) A brain like yours was never there in the entire past history and will never be there in the future (na bhootho, na bhavishyathi). Brains are continuously creating novelties.

– Guha

May 1, 2015
New Jersey

Today is a special day for us. It is Guha's birthday. With great enthusiasm I headed to 42 with a cake in hand and warm felicitations in mind. However, any ideas of a celebration soon vanished when Guha announced that this was just another day, no need to treat it any different. Looking at his somber expression there was no doubt he meant business. Last year, he had switched off his phone the entire day and no one could get through to him. Eager beavers like me, however, jammed poor Julie's phone line instead and reach him we did. U.G. too disliked such observances and made it crystal clear in a letter to his close friends who were keen to fete him, "Celebrating the birthday of anyone is an immature, childish, infantile activity.... You may spend your time in fasts, feasts and festivals, but leave this individual who has neither birth nor death severely alone ... ." Similarly, Ramana penned a four-line poem in response to his devotees' pleas:

You who wish to celebrate birthday
Seek first whence your birth
One's true birthday is when one
Enters that which transcends
Birth and death – the Eternal Being

Earlier, on my birthday I would quote this verse to fellow Ramana devotees because it sounded so wonderful – this whole idea of transcending birth and death to be one with the Eternal Being. That would be a true birth day indeed. I can imagine Guha wagging his finger and reprimanding me: *And how would you go about transcending birth and death? Through your enquiry? Fat chance! Ha, ha!* When I prodded Guha to comment on it, the answer I got completely shocked me: *Whatever makes you overcome the fear of death is good enough for you.*

It was shocking because the fear of death is exactly what is plaguing me lately. The mere thought of Nandini becoming old, infirm and her corpse being torched on the funeral pyre is terrifying. I see the black van inching closer day by day and I am petrified that the day is near when it will carry me away. I will be gone, just like a whiff of smoke. The whole shebang started when I lost two of my favorite aunts and my childhood buddy Sandip in quick succession. Sandip was more like a younger sibling to me as I had known him from the day he was born till the day he died, that is his entire life. We grew up in the same apartment block in Mumbai and were inseparables through much of our childhood. Later in life, we drifted apart but whenever our paths crossed it was as if there was no gap. A couple of days before his sudden death, not too far from where I live, I received a text message from him out of the blue. He wanted to know if everything was alright with me and was satisfied that all was hunky-dory on my end. The loop was closed. A bond cemented with genuine love and affection is forever, whether you are near or far. My dear aunts passed away due to old age but suffered a lot towards the end. With a heavy heart I turn to Guha for solace. He says, "Life is always changing form but there is no death. Death is not a property of life; change is. You are changing all the time. Today you are not the same person who fought with her mother when she was little." No sentiment there, just hard facts.

As we observe around us, Nature is in a state of constant flux. I have often heard Guha quote the Greek philosopher Heraclitus, "We both step and do not step in the same river" as it is continually flowing onwards. Change and death being ubiquitous features of our universe, entities are born, thrive for a time, degenerate and perish or change form. Within us also a similar process goes on – a thought is born, stays for a while and subsides, and another one sprouts up....so it continues ad infinitum. In Hindu scriptures, the entire cycle of creation, sustenance and destruction has been symbolized by a triad of principal gods, the Trimurti of Brahma the Creator, Vishnu the Sustainer and Shiva the Destroyer. Mysterious Nature, who can unravel thy secrets, mere mortals that we are, we can only philosophize and conceptualize.

Guha continues, "You cannot 'think' about death. You are afraid of the unknown, of something coming to an end. You translate death into a kind of void and that's what makes you afraid. That fear is bothering and interfering with your present living and creating a conflict in the living structure. You are always carrying the burden of that non-existing phenomenon. You witness other people dying around you, so you presume that there's death for you too and you are afraid of that. However, you will not be there to witness your own death. If you think 'you' will be there to witness that event, then also you are immortal. Either way, there is no death. Someone who cannot imagine about death cannot die or there is no death for him. To put it differently, if the question of death does not arise when I'm living then there's no death (for me)."

N: Is there any way out of this fear?
G: There is no way out, so the fear is always translated and expressed through the imaginative faculty. However, fear also has a component on the living structure. For example, if there's a tiger in front of you, your body has to respond to that threat. And the mechanism through which it responds – your imaginative fear – is the same mechanism, a powerful one.

We have something in our brain structure called mirror neurons which play a very important role. Suppose someone is lying mutilated and dead in front of you – the body must somehow respond to that. The system has some sort of protective mechanism for its own survival through that scene. Mirror neurons can make you translate the pain, fear and agony that the dying man is going through into your guts. And you are worried about it, you are scared about it and that is also important. It's the funny part about the living structure. It has some substantial fear which is extremely important for its own survival. And so, it needs to understand that and while doing so, through its imaginative faculty creates a scenario which is crucial for its survival. On the flip side, it also puts a burden on the system along with it. Something that is essential to understand extends beyond its necessity and leads to other problems. It's like our pleasure movement – you have a taste in your mouth and that's how you are propelled to eat. But then what happens? The sense of taste takes precedent over the necessity and you overeat. Thus, the sense of taste is important up to a certain extent but when it becomes the predominating factor it creates other problems, putting burden on the system.

Later, he graciously blew birthday candles and cut the cake. Happy Birthday, Guha.

May 2, 2015
New York City

After relishing a lavish meal made by Lakshmi, we all, Guha, Julie,

Lakshmi, Radhika, Ila and I have come to the city. We are here to greet a newcomer, a U.G. fan named Suresh N. He never met U.G. but wants to meet as many U.G. friends as possible. In his quest, Suresh has been traveling far and wide accompanied by his German girlfriend Diana. After his arrival in New York, he contacted Julie requesting a meeting.

As soon as the couple entered, I sensed that the gentleman was here on a mission, to fulfill an agenda. And the minute he opened his mouth it was evident that he wanted to spread the word how he had "got it" what U.G. was talking about. Things started to get a little nasty when he got into an unfriendly sparring match with Guha. He kept interrupting and contradicting Guha, liberally quoting JK, U.G., Narayana Moorty etc. to prove his point. Now I hear him ask Guha what his idea is about the mind. Guha looks stern and his tone is a little aggressive. I think he senses a kind of a wall, a closed door with the guest which makes him respond in such a way. In the back and forth, I hear words like "mind f…" masturbation, meditation, etc. flying around.

Suresh: U.G. somehow knocked out everything. Now consciously I'm not seeking anything. Why U.G.'s words impressed me was because I was stuck.

G: All words are produced by your mind. Words cannot remove the conditioning.

S: The sense of self is there, and it is not a problem for me.

G: So then nice meeting you and bye, bye!

Listening to them, I am reminded of my first "date" with Guha which was as different from this one as chalk and cheese. It was so much more congenial and sanguine since I had no intention to challenge him, only to clear my doubts. Plus, there were just three of us – Guha, Julie and I which was a relief. Prior to that, I was gobbling up U.G. books non-stop for several weeks. The more I read, the more anguished I was at the thought that I had missed the U.G. boat. The opportunity of meeting someone as fearless, outspoken and one-of-a-kind revolutionary thinker as U.G. was lost forever, I lamented to myself. Ironically, I was so close (yet so far) because I lived just ten minutes down the road from Julie whom he had visited several times. Of course, I had never heard of Julie or read U.G. at the time. It was hard to console myself, but my interest was piqued when in one of the books I came across an entire chapter devoted to Guha. It described the physical pain this New Jersey native had endured and a kind of metamorphosis that took place in his system after being with U.G. It also stated that he worked as a research scientist at Rutgers University and lived not too far from me.

Curioser and curioser, I Googled Guha's name and lo and behold, a website popped up almost instantaneously. Very excited, I skimmed through the pages several times in coming days looking for justification of my spiritual practices. I was sorely disappointed though as Guha debunked every notion or idea I valued. Nonetheless, there was a strange pull which I could not shrug off. But hankering after Guha was tantamount to admitting that there was something lacking in Ramana. On the other hand, I did not want to miss this chance either, like I had with U.G. The dilemma was resolved with the thought that would I not want to meet Ramana if he was alive, at least once? After some more procrastination, I gingerly penned a brief message to Golda, the webmaster. A few days later, I got the good news – Guha had agreed to see me! That fateful day was the winter solstice of 2013, December 21.

As soon as I entered Julie's house, I saw a thin, nerdy-looking Bengali Babu sitting alone on the couch, squinting at me through small, round glasses. Looks can be deceiving because he had such a ready wit and a hearty laugh that I dubbed him the Laughing Guha then and there. After the pleasantries, I opened the book on Ramana I had brought with me and read aloud a passage to him. It had to do with the wise man purportedly liberating his mother by keeping his hands on her chest when she was dying, thereby "liberating" her of all karmas. In Ramana's own words, *"The vasanas of the previous births and latent tendencies which are seeds of future births came out. She (mother) was observing one after another the scenes of experiences arising from remaining vasanas. As a result of a series of such experiences she was working them out."* Later, when someone asked Ramana to explain the process, he responded, *"Birth experiences are mental. Thinking is also like that, depending on samskaras (tendencies). Mother was made to undergo all her future births in a comparatively short time."* What did Guha have to say?

I don't recall Guha's specific answer to that question or for that matter anything he uttered that day. I just remember he was brief and said something to the effect that these were all stories and I chose to believe them. Anyway, I was amused that the minute he started talking, Julie who was sitting next to him, was out like a light, her head bobbing up and down. To my amazement, that is a recurring phenomenon every single time to this day. I went home and continued with my practices as if nothing extraordinary had happened. However, I could not forget Guha and thought he was quite original. As for Julie, I was a big fan of her book, *My Travels with U.G.* so was very happy to come face to face with this courageous lady. Next day, I sent them a polite note:

Dear Julie & Guhaji,

Thank you both so much for your time. I had a wonderful time yesterday and after a long time I met people whom I really felt at home with. I feel I can go on listening to Guhaji for hours and hours! He has such an authentic way of explaining things. And Julie you are truly a beautiful person – inside and out. Would it be possible to meet you – say a once a month on a regular basis? Maybe I could come and help you with stuff (I know you don't need my help, but it would give me a chance to spend time with you).

To this day Guha can't stop laughing at my silly email and tells all and sundry, "She said she wanted to see me only once a month! In fact, when I didn't hear from her, I had to ask Julie to write to her and went to meet her in Princeton myself!" Thank you, Guha, I would have been a lost chicken if you hadn't taken matters in your hands.

Later, when I again broached the topic of future births and reincarnation with Guha, he replied, "Reincarnation is a matter of one's belief structure. You can believe in anything." U.G. too had similar views on the subject declaring the whole concept of reincarnation was built on the foundation of belief. As such, there was no law of reincarnation like we have the law of gravity.

Q: If the belief structure itself is deemed as illusory then isn't the whole theory of reincarnation spurious?

Guha: Yes, it is self-contradictory. If the belief structure is spurious, so is your belief, isn't it? Whatever life needs to carry on, it is doing that. It matters not what you believe because your brain, a thinking brain, always pre-supposes a belief. That's the pattern of a thinking brain unless something radically changes inside. Then it always makes it believe as just a model; it is just for the sake of maintaining a social protocol. Your democracy is a belief structure, your political system is a belief structure.

There are certain experiences which can unfold in a human head and to explain those experiences someone must have a kind of a priori model. For instance, Buddha could not understand or logically explain his experience, so he had no choice but to invoke reincarnation in absence of advanced knowledge about brain functioning like we have today.

Q: When a person dies, what happens to that energy?

Guha: Nothing. The energy redistributes itself among other forms of life. There is dynamic energy and there is static energy. At death, dynamic energy called breathing stops and the body, which has tremendous amount of energy in terms of mass gets converted and is used by other life forms. Your knowledge and such things will be of no use then. That which was operating before you died will not be available anymore anywhere; it just stops. There is no oxygen coming to the body, creating energy from food and running the machine. The brain composition will decompose and become part of nature again. When you die, it becomes static energy because you are not absorbing anything or giving out anything. Again, when you are breathing, you are collecting energy, when you are eating you are collecting energy. So, the energy is being utilized. All that comes to a stop at death. If you throw a dead body into the garbage can, different animals will eat it up. They will consume that energy, proteins and everything from there. If you burn it, it will combine with other energies of the universe. The body is a living system and has to be available to other living systems. The energy will be distributed among all the bugs, bees, animals, trees et al. In short, everything goes back to nature. The total amount of energy in the universe always remains constant, merely changing from one form to another; it cannot be created or destroyed.

May 4, 2015

It is late evening and I have just returned home from an overnight road trip to Niagara Falls with Guha. In all, there were five of us with Julie, Lakshmi and Ila making up the rest of the party. It takes about eight hours to reach Niagara, a long ride. While I was pleased as punch to get this bonus time with Guha, I am tired and completely drained due to awful seasonal allergies. It is spring time here and the pollen from millions of blooming trees wreaks havoc with my system. I am miserable with a throbbing headache, stuffy nose, nonstop sneezing, and puffy, bloodshot, itchy eyes. No pill seems to give any relief but I am hoping a good night's sleep will do the trick. The web of life is so intricately woven that the macrocosm has a direct bearing on the microcosm, the living being, one way or another.

The outing was planned by Guha who wanted Ila to experience the falls, one of the seven Natural Wonders of the World. Surprisingly, Julie has never been here all her life but was pleasantly taken in by their magnificence. The weather was a little nippy with strong winds blowing but a ride on the *Maid of the Mist* was refreshing and rejuvenating. Perhaps the powerful, misty spray from the thundering falls will cleanse away all my "sins", I humor myself. Just like the Hindus who believe bathing in the Ganges washes away all your wrongdoings. Allergies apart, I was constantly on my toes around Guha as it can get intense without warning. Many a time I have been caught off guard because he comes out with the most perspicacious statements when you are least expecting it, like while cracking a joke or discussing the weather. It's no laughing matter, mind you.

Sitting in the Niagara Falls State Park Guha and I have the following discussion:

N: Where is humanity headed? Is there any hope for us?

G: The balance between the perceptive reality and the imaginative faculty of the human mind will be achieved but only after a catastrophic event. I had several visions of enormous destruction all around. Human beings will be forced to align with Nature for their own survival. Mere knowledge cannot bring about order.

N: Did life begin from Adam and Eve?

G: That is a simplified model born out of somebody's imagination.

N: So, we will have something like Ram Rajya after the catastrophic event?

G (exclaims): There was never any Ram Rajya where people lived in peace and harmony. It is a story. In fact, human beings were very violent, more so than now. As I said, humans will be forced to align with Nature after a holocaust.

He adds, "Is it possible to find your own natural existence? By yourself you are very different from when you are in a group. It creates a distorted reality. The momentum inside you keeps driving you to participate in the social dynamics. It is like a drug. But your system originally didn't want it. It is human arrogance to control life. You dominate (and control) your kids. But there is no choice, for if you don't then others will dominate them. There is no way out. In this society you have no choice but to play this game. Or you can sink in despair and kill yourself. Or kill others. But if you truly understand what I am saying you have no right to kill yourself. The being that thinks it has the right to kill the host is false! That being, "I" false! It is using wrong knowledge for the wrong end."

On the return trip, we took our first break at the Corning factory store, famous for its Corelle tableware as well as the glass museum. It is a ritual among Corelle-crazy *desis* to visit this outlet without fail to stack up on their glassware, bakeware and dishware. We too were overjoyed to find great bargains and stuffed our bags with curios, plates, bowls and cups.

May 6, 2015
Morning

We are heading to the city and I am feeling alert, unlike the tamasic stupor I frequently find myself in. Guha is in a fierce mood, no time for frivolities. I feel his vibes and am ready to make the most of it. I quickly ask him some questions about human life to get him going:

- *Nature expresses itself through different species. Everything is already here from beginning till the end. There is nothing new. You are as much an expression of Nature as me.*
- *All seeds have the potential to become a tree, but do they become? No. Can any scientist tell you which seeds will become trees in the future by mathematical calculations? No. Life is also like that. It's all chance.*
- *The egg that would become you was already there in your grandmother's womb, especially the female egg. When a female fetus is there in mother's womb, she is already having the egg sequences to be born.*
- *Every single life form is threatened because it is being challenged, devoured by other life forms. We don't have any choice but to accept and respond to that challenge. The organism's innate programming*

is survival and procreation. To do that, it must respond to the challenge by creating capacities. The power of life is creating these capacities – giraffes have long necks, tigers get claws, etc. One of the capacities that came to this biped animal is thinking. This capacity has a peculiarity – it can create a very illusory, mythical structure and live in that. This thinking capacity gives us an advantage over other species. It can think and reflect about life beyond stimulus and response. Thinking itself is outside the framework of stimulus and response.

- *Life's intelligence is constantly creating novel capacities; there is no central programmer or an executive director who's doing this.*
- *The powerful force which created this machine (the intellect) has a lot of Nature's power and logic behind it which makes you perceive things in life. Through that logic you can see a lot and do a lot. But you try to extrapolate. You go to a different regime and it doesn't work.*
- *What is it that you want? If you want happiness you have to know the meaning of happiness. If you want to have self-satisfaction with another person, then you must know that it involves another person's desire pattern. Basically, you are solo.*

As we neared Holland Tunnel, Guha fell quiet as there was a big traffic jam near the entrance. A car was blocking one lane due to a tire puncture. Julie, referring to present day gurus in general, cried out in jest, "They can't even change a flat tire, let alone change anybody!" Incidentally, Guha is more than adept at changing a flat.

It is evening and we are huddled together at Julie's. Lest I forget, I bring up our conversation from Niagara, "You mentioned yesterday about humans aligning with Nature after a catastrophic event …. Does it mean that people will be more sattvic and will be able to easily grasp the reality?" Guha laughs, "You don't need to be sattvic to grasp reality!" I dropped the topic for now.

Guha and Radhika start bantering:

R: Just because I say I want something or if I say I don't want something it doesn't make any difference.
G: Then why do you do the things you do?
R: That's my conditioning. That's how it comes out. What can I do?
G: If you think nothing's in your hand then don't do anything. What is it that you are seeking or wanting?
R: I don't know.
G: Then go home and do what you can do.
R: That's not much fun.
G: I'm not an entertainer!
Ouch. Be ready for anything for you never know what's going to hit you.

~

Chapter Ten

Butterflies Are Free

There is no such thing as self in the real sense since 'I' is nothing but a set of knowledge. My world, the world that I know is based on that knowledge center. So, 'I' being the source of illusion, everything we know is an illusion. Because that what we have already accepted as standard from where I understand everything is based on an assumption, everything is a measurement. That's the measurement. The existence of the center of measurement itself is an illusion. So without self, there is no understanding. That is how the whole idea of illusion came about. That is how the word maya came. Everything is with respect to the knowledge center of an individual. That's why the world is maya, not the way it exists for this animal but how it exists for the knower, the one who knows, the one who understands.

– Guha

June 1, 2015
New Jersey

We are in 42, Guha's home, chatting about this, that or the other. Since his house number is 42 it has become a habit for us to address this location as just 42. Recently, someone informed us that in the wildly popular science fiction series *Hitchhiker's Guide to the*

Galaxy, "The answer to the ultimate question of life, the universe and everything is 42." No kidding!

Manoj's stay here is coming to an end very soon and he is preparing himself for the inevitable, "Guha, how can I get a piece of you when I am back home?" Guha answers, "You don't need it, that's why you don't get it. It's all complete at the inception." After a pause, he continues, "Remembrance is always in terms of thoughts and memories. U.G. made it clear that there was nothing in my memory that had any importance to the energy I was dealing with… I could trash in one second everything. The powerful energy beating through your guts like there's no tomorrow burns everything. Dead bodies (saints, sages) are just ideas, images. If I know those ideas don't match the way life is functioning, then they are useless." He adds, "When you do not try to control your environment then you are free, you are symbiotically connected with life."

Turning to Radhika, "You are not interested in what I'm saying." She argues how he is so sure of that. He replies, "Everything about you tells me that. What you are interested in is to earn money, earn fame, seek pleasure, etc. Whether you sit here or go home it makes no difference; might as well earn money. If you are really honest you will ask yourself what your interest is."

Radhika retorts, "You wouldn't engage with somebody if you didn't think they were really interested in what you have to say." Guha laughs, "What a clever mind you have and what a beautiful justification."

Guha is in a talkative mood and as my mind wanders, I catch phrases like power of delusion having no limits, doing seva, worshiping images, becoming a bonded slave, emancipation, subject specific functional reality and so on. And then this, "Your concern is how your core conflict is addressed by your system. Thought and logical thinking have no meaning for the freedom you are seeking. U.G. used to say even a dog knows how to go back home to his master. At the end of the day, you will find yourself on your two little feet which are sooooo strongly grounded."

Now he's making small talk with Revathi on the phone. After the call, he says there are snake-like swellings around her neck at times. Many years ago, while Revathi was visiting Africa a mamba snake walked over her feet. Locals believe it is very rare that someone can come out alive after such an incident. This led Shujaat, the jokester in Guha court, to dub her Mambadevi. Moreover, Revathi hails from Mumbai whose patron deity is Mumbadevi, so the name has stuck.

Radhika: Explain what you mean by there's no such thing as truth.

Guha: Thought cannot capture the living moments of life. That is the only truth. Everything else is just an idea, a concept. We have accepted certain things as truth, that's all. For example, we have divided time into B.C. and A.D. Can you call that truth? Everything is like that.

Manoj keeps butting in while Radhika and Guha are busy talking. A little annoyed, Radhika remonstrates him, "Manoj, stop it. *Aap kyon hamesha damroo bajate rahte ho?*" (Why are you are always playing the damru (a small two-headed drum))?

Manoj (ignoring her): Guha, when I say I see you, is that the truth?

Guha: No, it is not. Can you call it truth? Then you have to get down to semantics. Who is looking, who is seen, etc.? Can you look at anything without having an idea about it?

Manoj: I have no way of looking at you except through the knowledge I have about you. How true is the Vedic statement, "Brahma satya, jagat mithya?" (Brahman is truth, manifest universe is false)

Guha: Jagat is what is in front of you. Any idea you have about jagat is maya.

U.G. and Guha attributed maya to measurement and I want to know what exactly it means. Guha obliges, "In physics, everything that we want to know is with respect to something. For example, if I want to know how far it is from here to there, you have to compare. What does it mean when I say from here to there, in terms of what? So, we invent a unit called a foot or a meter. Then we give it a definition. That is a comparison. First, you define something and then compare it with that which you have defined. It is a state of comparison. All experiences are with respect to what you already know, what you feel. That's why the word maya came from measurement. It is not illusion. How do you say 'I am perceiving' without using something that you already understand? In the same way, you have some unit of understanding the way you have been conditioned from childhood to say things. Since you were a baby, mom told you what is what, like the color red. Since you have already been given the word and its meaning, you always match it, just the way you measure.

"Every experience is a state of measurement. That's maya. Now you do that automatically, spontaneously because it is already set up. The moment you want to talk about your experience it is with respect to your conditioning.... Anything you experience must have a measurement. That's why what you see is an absolute necessity for the organism. What you think you are seeing, without that measurement, without that illusory aspect of your knowledge, you cannot know. What you think you are seeing, what you think you have experienced, what you think you have dreamed are all under the name of maya. All relationships too fall under that, sorry. It's a measurement. I cannot exist without this measurement. If you say 'I', it has no meaning. I am R, R, N, K. Thinking cannot produce, thinking cannot progress without that object.

"The subject 'I' cannot exist without an object. Really, it is the object which is creating the subject. Sometimes thinking about yourself itself IS the object. You need food for your thought. What is thought? I am good, I am bad, I am suffering, I am happy, I want this, I want that, I want to see myself in such and such image, etc. So, you are thinking about yourself. To continue this 'I' it needs some measurement, a connection. This has been going on since childhood and has become such an automation that you don't have to do a thing. *Gaddi apne aap chal rahi hai. Tel kaun de raha hai?* (The train is running by itself. Who is giving it fuel?) Your energy. Reality doesn't exist. There's only functional reality of the social structure."

June 2, 2015

Guha is regaling us with anecdotes about his friends this afternoon. His innocent, child-like enactments interlaced with animated gestures evoke lots of laughter and conjure up vivid images in my mind. I remember his master performance of a drunken character a few weeks ago. Jumping to his feet, he swayed, staggered and stumbled as if he were on a ship in stormy seas. Then, pretending to lose his balance fell on his seat with a thump! I was so tickled watching the act that I begged him to repeat it, which to my delight he did with the same gusto. I have seen him in many different moods such as being ferocious like a tiger when he is really animated or charged up about something or as soft as a kitten when remembering his mother. Moreover, I have observed a strange phenomenon taking place in my system when I am in Guha's proximity. I am chirpy and ebullient initially but as the day wears on, my internal machinery seems to slow down with no energy left to ask any more questions or participate in any discussion. Sometimes I fall asleep, his voice a soothing lullaby transporting me to la la land. Lately, when I am sitting next to him, I feel a rush of heat in my body and it is so intense at times that I have to get up and move away otherwise I would pass out. It's a roller coaster ride being with Guha, no doubt. But I digress. Let's hear the stories.

Balaram was introduced to Guha in 2010 by his friend Ramakrishna Chatterjee who was Guha's schoolmate. Now retired, he worked as a motor mechanic in Hindustan Motors in Guha's hometown, Hind Motor. Once, this jovial, down-to-earth and unpretentious soul was inspired to write a poem in praise of Guha. Never having penned a verse in his entire life, he nonetheless composed a paean in which he depicted Guha as "Prajapati". In Sanskrit, the term means Lord of Humanity but in Bengali it also means a butterfly. He then thought of getting his piece examined by an expert since he was a novice writer. With that in mind, he approached a buddy who was a literary critic. After looking through it, the pundit advised Balaram to replace the word "Prajapati" with "Dhruv Tara" (Pole Star) as perhaps he felt the former was too grand to describe Guha. Even though not too pleased with the suggestion, Balaram did as he was instructed. When he reached home that night, he was dumbstruck to find his entire bedroom filled with tiny butterflies. Terrified by the thousands of winged creatures fluttering around him, he ran outside and called Ramakrishna. After listening to Balaram's "horror" story, Ramakrishna advised him to reinstate "Prajapati" immediately.

Here is the Bengali transliteration followed by English translation by Ramakrishna:

Gobhir moner bhitar hotey likhlam prothom dekhaar onubhuti.
Sokoler majhkhane tumi holey ek projapoti.
Kato maanusher korey thaako tumi sadgoti.
Ei biswas aachhe sakal maanush jaatir
Aamraa haa korey sabaai bosey khaali bhaabi
Ekbar tumi ki chhnuye jaabe naaki
Naa chhuleo antorer bhetor ekta asha jaage
Tumi to royechho amader sakoler majhkhane
Eo kom noy tomar kaache paoa
Sudhu jaoar samoy diye jeo santona.

Prajapati

These are the words deep from my heart, a feeling when I first met you.
You are the PRAJAPATI amongst us, true.
You have done for so many the right things
People from all nations believe this.
We are overwhelmed yet waiting with our jaws open by the thought
That perhaps you will touch us all.

Even if not, hope arises from within,
That you are nonetheless there amongst us,
Even this is not a small thing to get.
Please give a little solace when you leave us.

Once Balaram was in a bit of a jam over a family dispute and had to rush to his village on a summons. His sister-in-law had filed a court case related to their ancestral property and he was ordered to be at the police station to sign some important documents. He was deeply perturbed at being pushed to do so against his will but could see no way out. During the train journey, he started reading Guha's Bengali book *14 Days in Palm Springs with U.G.* to keep his mind occupied. For Balaram, that little book was his Bible which he always carried with him wherever he went. Here's when the plot thickens. He reaches his destination, starts walking towards the police station but senses that something is not right. People are giving him strange looks. Before he arrives at the *thana,* he gets the big news - the lady who had been giving him so much grief had died unexpectedly the previous night.

Taposh is a school teacher and a poet who befriended Guha through his poet friend Swapan Babu who is a distant relative of Guha. In fact, when Luna Tarlo, Guha's author friend from New York, met Swapan she was so impressed by his talents that she named him the Bengali Edgar Allen Poe. When Taposh was introduced to Guha, he was mourning the death of his girlfriend who had succumbed to cancer recently. Overcome with grief and sadness he was going through severe depression, was unable to write or work and generally kept to himself. Barely acknowledging Guha's presence, he sat in a corner far away, not participating in the talks. After a while, he suddenly sprang to his feet and announced loudly, "I will eat something now!" When everyone was leaving, Guha took him aside and gifted him a Swarovski pen. That night when he was appreciating the glittering pen, Taposh felt a burning sensation in his hand and the muse began to flow. Then and there he sat down at his desk and worked through the night. Before dawn he had composed three poems and in three months he had penned a hundred verses. To his amazement, he even won a prestigious literary award for his creations. What a priceless gift from a perfect stranger. I think upon meeting Guha his pent-up emotions were released and he was back on track almost instantly. Later, he met his current wife and began a new life in Jalpaiguri in North Bengal.

In his ancestral home in Hind Motor, Guha's brother had rented out a portion of the house to a young couple. They were eagerly waiting to see Guha having heard a lot about him from their landlord. When Guha arrived, they wasted no time in inviting him to their place but to no avail as Guha kept refusing. After several more attempts, their persistence paid off as Guha finally agreed to visit them. As soon as he entered their quarters, he recognized the familiar room; it was here that he had spent most of his childhood. After exchanging pleasantries, the lady of the house proceeded to narrate her plight. They had been married for seven years but had not begot any children. They wanted Guha to bless them with a child. Guha thought to himself, *oh my god, what have I gotten myself into?* Anyway, he urged the couple to consult a doctor right away assuring them that, if anything, scientific advances in fertility technology could help them fulfill their wish. He reiterated that medical science had progressed by leaps and bounds in the last decade which would surely help her conceive. What a practical advice that was. If they had approached a "holy man", he would have emptied their pockets by giving them some bogus mantra, tantra and put them on a merry-go-round of false hopes. The following year when he was back he met the beaming couple and the mother proudly held up her bundle of joy for Guha to admire.

Then there were Peter, Paul and Mary battling Mercy the merciless. The goodwill trio was Guha's colleagues and supervisors at Rutgers University who broke all rules and protocols in getting him the US Green Card in the nick of time. Guha was on a temporary work permit and if he did not get the GC he and his family would have to pack their bags and say bye, bye to Uncle Sam. Mercy was the college attorney in charge of processing immigration visas and Green Cards for the faculty. She refused to touch Guha's case because the time for filing had passed long ago and under no circumstances was she willing to bend the rules. By now, Guha was at his wit's end with no solution in sight. A couple of days later, Paul came running to him and declared that Mercy's entire department had been dissolved by the college! Guha's path was cleared and he got his GC within one month.

June 4, 2015
At 42

Julie, Radhika, Kishor and Manoj are all here discussing Arunachala and Tiruvannamalai. Guha looks at me and says, "Your faith in Arunachala and Ramana is strengthening and fortifying the sense of self, the 'I' in you. If anyone can't understand that they haven't understood how the mechanism of mind works."

As all close friends of Guha know, Manoj and I are always clashing over anything and everything related to Guha. This started in 2014 when I was in Cochin and has been continuing ever since. He is of the opinion that I demand exclusive attention from Guha and thinks it is his right and duty to prevent me from monopolizing him. Sometimes it is just light bantering or trading barbs but at times it can get nasty, like today. While I was trying to get some answers from Guha, he kept interrupting us repeatedly which got my goat and I snapped at him to stop acting like a "chaprasi". Actually and factually, I wanted to say "darwan", meaning a doorman or a gate keeper (for Guha) but in my agitation, I inadvertently used the word "chaprasi" which means a peon in Hindi. Guha chided me that the term "chaprasi" was a little demeaning. However, not to be outdone,

Manoj's swift rejoinder was if he was a "chaprasi", I was a racist B-I-T-C-H! The sheer vehemence with which he uttered the word BITCH was disturbing and a new experience since I have never ever been called a bitch to my face. But why should I be crestfallen? Reacting to compliments or condemnations only strengthens my sense of identity, right Guha? From now onwards no more wasting time on such juvenile activities. K had already warned me several times to refrain from doing so, admonishing me mildly, "It's not very healthy to indulge in such slanging matches as beyond a point it is an intolerable waste of energy."

June 6, 2015

I have said it before and I reiterate again – the one thing I truly want is to be totally free from being emotionally dependent on anybody, how much ever I may love them. That's what I really want, from the bottom of my heart. I tell Guha it's not a good feeling to show weakness and be a slave to someone else's desires and whims. He agrees.

Yesterday we were just driving aimlessly around town, happy to have Guha in our midst. After a while, we stopped at a Starbucks for an evening cupper. While I was talking to Guha, Manoj again kept interrupting us and passing some snide remarks like I needed a new head, I was always lost, etc. This time I was wiser and kept quiet. Later, Guha pulled me aside and said, "Don't let anyone come between you and me in your head. Do you understand? In your head. Anyone can say or do anything. That doesn't make any difference."

June 7, 2015
New York City

We drove to Ansonia this morning and after a quick lunch we are on our way to Brooklyn where we have been invited by a U.G. friend, Louis Brawley who is an artist and a writer. He is holding an exhibition of his paintings this weekend. Matt, Guha, Radhika and I are in Matt's car followed by Shujaat, Kishor and Manoj in Shujaat's car. I hear Guha and Matt talking softly in the front: "When you do not use anybody to please yourself, then you are free." We cruise slowly through the city, cross over Manhattan Bridge and are on a busy, noisy, straight-as-an-arrow roadway called Broadway Avenue. Later, I got an earful from Louis, "I am about to give you a lecture about Broadway, that it is never called Broadway Avenue, but as it turns out, it is an avenue, but no one ever calls it Broadway Avenue, simply Broadway. I think that's a habit that comes from the Manhattan Broadway usage." Broadway is humming with shoppers and pedestrians, cars whizzing by blaring loud music, and the subway trains roaring overhead on elevated tracks. There is an abundance of pawn shops, thrift shops, smoke shops, consignment shops, clothing stores, shoe shops, restaurants and cafes lining both sides of the broad road. Names like Fat Albert, Urban Jungle and Super Runners catch my eye as we speed along. This reminds me of Colaba in Mumbai, home to the famed Gateway of India monument on the waterfront. The main Colaba area is choc-a-bloc with rows of restaurants, boutiques, shops of all hues and street vendors hawking trinkets, housewares, footwear, cheap clothing and what have you. It is one of the oldest shopping and tourist spots in Mumbai where you can find foreigners and locals alike hanging out in the iconic Leopold or Mondegar cafes or roaming the streets hunting for bargains.

Louis' apartment-cum-studio is right on Broadway on top of a Chinese restaurant. For some unknown reason they call the building "Hotel" and most of the occupants are artists like him. Today is Open Studio Day at the Hotel and residents have thrown their doors open to art aficionados and showcase their talents. It seems Brooklyn is fast becoming the go-to place to buy art. This weekend alone there are over 700 listings of art shows. I go around the room admiring Louis' work. Although I don't understand art, I like what I see; Louis' paintings have an esoteric feel. If I had the money, I would have bought a couple. In the background, I hear the subway train screeching by every few minutes since his apartment is on level with the tracks. I should call him Saint Louis for enduring such a racket day in day out! I laugh at Louis' candid confession, "...my 'saintly' life bearing the racket beneath the roaring M train... the fact is that roaring is a perfect metaphor for the most un-saintly racket in my head... so maybe it's helpful."

U.G. had a huge impact on Louis whose widely read book *Goner* "represents my encounter with one of the most unique and elusive figures outside of any school of thought". As for his paintings, he admits, "The ideas for most of my work (oil and watercolor) these days come from an obsession with painting, literature, extended exposure to Indian philosophies, and a man called U.G. Krishnamurti...." U.G. always discouraged him to paint saying he was a "horrible painter" and encouraged him to write more instead. I though admire him for both his talents. Louis is also a close friend of Guha and his entire family. I meet him from time to time either at Guha's or in the city. I will always be thankful to him for helping me to get this journal off ground.

Back at Ansonia, Guha, Radhika and I are having evening tea/ coffee. Guha says everyone is reading the English translation of *14 Days in Palm Springs with U.G.* I confess to him that I had not read it since I did not have the translation. He casually remarks that I am not interested in reading it. That is true because I am not motivated to read anything nowadays. He adds, just like the dream I had, I am wishy washy, that I don't seem to be interested. Then he turns the knife, saying softly, *maybe I have a different calling*. I do not utter a word as no answer is forthcoming. After all, what can I say? Many a time I feel his attacks are unjust; perhaps he can enlighten me on this one and tell me what my calling is. I myself don't know, Guha.

The dream he was referring to was about Guha, of course. He was sitting in my TV room on the couch underneath the window and the lights above the TV were on, but the room appeared dark.

Guha asked me to turn on the lights above him. I flipped the switch, but nothing happened. No light. Next, I tried the kitchen light. Same thing. Then I found myself in the garage, opening the box where all the switches are housed trying to see if any of them had tripped. At that point I woke up. Later, when I narrated the dream to Guha, he said it was feeble, had no energy.

June 8, 2015

As soon as I woke up, the first thing I did was text Guha asking him what time I could go see him. I instantly got a ping, "You don't mean it!" When I saw those words glaring at me, something snapped inside, and tears filled my eyes. I began to cry like a baby and the mind went into a total frenzy with all sorts of horrible thoughts rearing their ugly heads. *I am fed up trying to defend myself every time. I DO mean what I say. I'm not going to call him! I'll go retire in a corner alone and swear will never meet him or anybody. I'm done!* As if I meant any of that. As soon as the storm passed and calm prevailed, I again wrote to Guha. It took a lot of will power to do so but I had to express myself clearly, "I am saying I want to meet you, you are saying I don't. I have no way of defending your statement. In my hearts of heart, I know I'm not lying. You tell me what you want me to do and I'll respect that." He must have sensed my anguish for he immediately replied, "Okay, thank you dear." After that it was sugar and spice and everything nice! He even called and spoke to me at length. He said I must one-pointedly gravitate towards that which addresses my core well-being. He gave an analogy of a waterfall in a jungle where all kinds of animals gather to drink water. Even if the jungle is full of ugly, dangerous animals, we still have to devise a way to reach the water. I get the point. I described the whole incident to K who listened to my rhetoric with his legendary patience. Blues gone, I cheerfully spent the rest of the day talking to him on the phone. We both feel the need to stay connected.

June 10, 2015

Early morning, I had another dream. This time there was a venomous snake staring at me from a distance. The greenish, black serpent looked threatening with its big fangs. There were two others with me but could not make out who they were. Perhaps one of them was my son. Anyway, we were huddled together in fright, our eyes fixed on the reptile waiting to see in which direction it would go. To our dismay, it began to slither towards us. My heart pounding, I closed my eyes tightly waiting for the lethal bite. But the sting never happened. In the next frame, the snake was hiding under a piece of furniture in my old house in Mumbai where I grew up. Even after a desperate search we could not find it. I woke up, the fright still lingering. I promptly narrated the dream to Guha who listened closely. "Next time it is going to bite you," he warned.

~

Chapter Eleven

Two Good Men

There is no aggression, that's the difference now. There is no Fascist nature (in me). I am just protecting myself, which is a big shift. The intentionality has completely changed. The aggression is gone but there is a powerful force which is protecting itself from the invasion of ideas and thoughts. I don't feel like influencing anybody. I have no impetus to spread my ideology. No such grandiose ideas are there. I communicate from what I call "information space". I have a very specific proprioception of thought itself. Thoughts are there with a very specific tag, with their reflexes. And I – 'I' means my intention- is to not allow these reflexes to change or be hijacked by other ideas. If you ask me what it is that is holding them together, I have no answer. It is information by itself, for itself. There is no impetus to propagate anything; it is only there to protect the organism. That is also a kind of a model. I have no power to perceive what is happening inside me. This is the best I can do to describe how I am functioning.

You can say anything but as far as I'm concerned, mental causation is still mysterious. The system is holding on to the unknown. It protects itself from invasion of ideas so that information cannot again form a structure and run the show. Since there is no structure, there is no so-called "center". The organism doesn't allow this to happen. I have experienced it many times. So, when I am getting involved in a very specific idea that I feel is superior, when I feel this is the way it should go, when I try to understand and put attributes to it, my brain rejects it. It gives me a big headache, a big pain, a big volcanic eruption inside me until that is completely smashed from inside. It's not peace, it's WAR! War against what? The physical organism itself is trying to sort it out, it will heat up, balance the neurotransmitter, cut, cut, cut the circuitry and I will have a peculiar pain and feeling, you know, and many times I'm 'gone' at night. Suddenly, the whole thing starts paining from the center of my navel and starts spreading in my body and I am choked as if something is imploding and squeezing me. Finished! It never allows the information structure to have a very specific idea to propagate. That's the big shift. So, what happens? I often feel helpless if somebody asks what's my idea? I don't know. What do I say? What's the point you're trying to make, they ask? None. People lose interest as there is no benefit. For the first time I came to know there's another way of living by the organism itself.

– Guha

June 11, 2015
New Jersey

Our friend Kishor is leaving for Mumbai today. I have come early to 42 to spend one last day with him and see him off at the airport later in the afternoon. Carol from South Carolina is also here visiting Guha for a few days. Right now she is mighty peeved with Manoj and his argumentative ways. She whispers in my ears how he got to be that way.

Guha: What are you saying, Carol? I want to hear it.

Carol: How did he (pointing to Manoj) get to this state of mind?

G: By listening to U.G. time and time again. He's following U.G.'s teachings better than most.

C: That's an example of U.G.'s teachings? This (he) is the end result of listening to U.G.?

G: No, not the end result.

C: The middle result, the beginning result?
G: He's one of the most genuine guys.
C: That's why he's so irritating? Oh, you're saying he's genuine but that's not the truth. He's a very irritating type. He's like the Christians – they have no good arguments, but they will keep saying, 'Have you read the Bible?' to shut you up. They will quote from the Bible when they can't prove anything. He (Manoj) is so argumentative, he doesn't listen at all. You're saying you like him?
G: I didn't say I like him. I said he is standing on his two little feet better than most people.
Manoj: She (Carol) wants to burn me to "bhasma" (ashes)!
C: You only got the best of it because he (Guha) is on your side which doesn't make any sense to me.

At the end of this waspish exchange, Carol was even more upset than at the beginning.

The vivacious, bubbly, theatrical, the one and only Carol is someone whom I can't help but love. The septuagenarian had a conservative upbringing being raised by Catholic nuns but her free spirit was never tamed. Perhaps that non-conformist streak coupled with a strong inclination towards spirituality led her to look for a deeper meaning in life in unconventional ways. While in her twenties, she came across the teachings of Kirpal Singh, founder of Ruhani Satsang, and followed his Path of the Masters with all her heart and soul. In those days it was not that easy to travel to India, but this brave lady did so several times to be with her beloved master. She felt a deep connection with the guru and even after all these years has tears in her eyes whenever she talks about him. Kirpal Singh passed away in 1974 and his son Master Darshan Singh took over as his successor. Carol stuck on with him too. After he died in 1989, his son Rajinder Singh took over the reins of the Satsang. That was when Carol left the Path as "the outer connection wavered".

Even with the Satsang link broken, Carol was not the one to give up her search. She began to research on present day gurus online but no one interested her until she came across U.G. Krishnamurti. She read all his books and watched umpteen U.G. videos on YouTube which she said were very impressive. After more research and many more clicks she found Guha. In her words, "he looked different from the rest" and resolved to meet him as soon as possible. She contacted Golda, webmaster of Guha's site, who put her in touch with Julie. After several back and forth, some misgivings and dire warnings from her children that she could land herself in a cult and be thrown into a dungeon, Carol found herself at Guha's doorstep. From her first meeting in 42 where she says she had an awkward meal with Guha, to the present, Carol, in her inimitable way has only deepened her connection with Guha while remaining steadfast in her reverence and devotion towards him.

In Carol's own words, *"It is impossible to speak of the details in the awareness unfolding in a person in the Presence of Guha. It would or could take volumes or maybe, simply a single word. Over time when we met in 2013 to 2017, all loose ends to the story in this Life of mine have come together and lovingly been put to rest. A daring and powerful explanation might be a quote from Sri Ramakrishna, who would say, "He is the Personal and Impersonal Manifestation of God Himself. ... To my lowly self, He is my end to the RIDDLE of LIFE."*

June 13, 2015

On this Saturday morning the whole gang is at Julie's waiting for a newcomer named Nish to arrive – Guha, Radhika, Revathi, Carol, Manoj, Shujaat, Julie and me. Nish has been reading U.G. books since 1998 but never met him, said he was afraid to do so. Like most of us, he found Guha through the same virtual route. Reading U.G. online, intrigued to learn about physical "changes" in someone named Guha, Googling "Guha" and viola, a "hit"! Here he is now shaking hands with G. Nish seems friendly and amiable but has a sharp mind. He is bursting with questions and wants to discuss everything from "disease to divinity" with Guha.

Revathi is looking a little pale as she is having a bad headache and reluctantly went upstairs to lie down. She says there was "significant shake-up" in her system after her momentous meeting with Guha in Chicago last January. The process has been continuing ever since. She has known Guha for many years but the windy city visit "was the proverbial last straw that broke the camel's back". She suffers from severe headaches and other pain, making it very hard for her to hold a full time job.

I have heard of people undergoing identical symptoms or experiences to those they are closely aligned with or resonate deeply with, such as gurus, mentors, close friends or lovers. For example, I read about a husband undergoing the same symptoms of pregnancy alongside his spouse or two female companions beginning their menstrual period on the same day despite having different cycles. I even heard of a father who was having a severe stomach pain and his daughter exhibiting similar symptoms at the same exact time even though they were living seven seas apart. How mysterious that such close connections can be established between two human beings, many times from different walks of life? However, in Revathi's case, whatever she is undergoing, could that be due to the superconducting proximity effect theory which Guha talks about all the time? Only Revathi can answer that. Guha never tires to explain this term to us as many times as we ask him. According to this theory, when a superconductor comes in close contact with a non-superconductor some strange phenomena can be observed in the latter. Guha believes that unusual things happened to him in U.G.'s (superconductor) presence.

I notice that Guha is wearing the same light blue shirt with white stripes which he was wearing the day before yesterday when Revathi arrived. He may have worn it yesterday too, but I did not meet him so can't say. Revathi gave it to him in Carol's house when we were all down in South Carolina a few months ago. He wore it for four days straight. It was the same with the green kurta that Kamal gifted to him when he was in New York recently. Guha wore the eye-catching tunic from Fab India boutique for three days in a row. When I pointed out to Guha that he must have liked it a lot, he replied it all depended on who gifted it. But wait, what impels me to take cognizance of such things? Clouds of envy, fear, insecurity passing by, may be? All this emotional dross leaves me exhausted and drained.

More dark clouds foreboding gloom and doom – some miscommunication with Guha threw me completely off balance and my mind was engulfed in negative, mistrustful thoughts. He must have sensed what I was going through because he specially called to explain that due to cell phone signal problem he could not get in touch with me earlier. He even persuaded me to meet him in Princeton that evening. At night, when I sent him a contrite note and apologized for being peevish and oversensitive over a trifle, he implored me never to treat myself so callously. He said he felt my torment in his guts. When I read his message, tears welled up in my eyes and I felt very sorry for myself. He was right; I should never be so hard on myself. Sometimes it is difficult to fathom Guha's ways and there are times when I misjudge him but he always proves me wrong. He is one genuine friend who knows what makes me tick and without judging, endeavors to help me. Each and every time.

Talking about friends, meeting Guha was like someone who was looking for a piece of rock but found a priceless gem instead. In fact, I was not even looking but the stars were smiling down on me; my time had come. The decade preceding the pivot was full of strife, sorrow and separation. At forty, my marriage was in the doldrums and I was in deep pain. I had lost all interest in life and was barely even talking to anyone. The already strained relationship with my husband took a turn for worse, no, reached its nadir, when he decided to throw me a 40th birthday party.

When we moved to the US in 1995, our first home was a small

apartment in a rental community. There I became acquainted with my neighbor Rajni. Our husbands worked in IT for big banks in New York and took the train to the city every day. Rajni had a daughter who was the same age as my son, both toddlers, so that was a big boon. Soon we became fast friends albeit our backgrounds were very different. She took me under her wing and made adjusting to my new life a breeze. From teaching me to be a savvy shopper, giving demos on north Indian cooking, introducing me to her desi friend circle and even helping me with driving lessons, I could not be happier to have her around. If the weather was good, we would put the babies in strollers and go for walks around the neighborhood. Sometimes we would take them to Chuck-e-Cheese's or to the malls. On weekends, along with our husbands we would go out dining, on picnics, day trips or to desi get-togethers. Our friendship continued even after we moved out of the rental complex and lived afar.

One day my husband decided to throw me a surprise birthday party and enlisted Rajni's help. To plan for the event, he drove over to her house without my knowledge. Being a weekday, Rajni's husband was at work and she was home alone. At this point, I must add that my husband had a roving eye but nothing too crazy barring a couple of minor incidents at workplace. Anyway, on that day god alone knows what came over him but he allegedly made advances towards her and kissed her against her will. Totally stunned and appalled by his audacious behavior, she was fearful to tell her husband. But there was no choice; she had to, to save her marriage. That night, all hell broke loose. Rajni's husband was livid, I was in shock and my husband cried and cried. Luckily, my little boy slept through the entire drama. Next morning, my bosom buddy's spouse gathered all his friends in a park, made my husband apologize to his wife on his knees, thrashed him in public and almost broke his arms. I was not present and never saw Rajni again.

This was the highlight of my 40th year. I did not have the courage to walk out even though I knew enough was enough. By now the marriage was in name only, there was no communication whatsoever between us, just tense silence, bitter resentment and anger boiling in the pit of my stomach. It continued in this fashion till by chance someone handed me a copy of the *Bhagavad Gita.* It undoubtedly lit a spark and gave me hope of "liberation", an escape route from suffering. Thus, began an intense phase of religiosity - meditation, japa, yoga, devotional activities and pilgrimages. Although my practices gave me some solace and purpose in life, there was no sign of any liberation. I turned to Nisargadatta Maharaj and *I Am That* which I read from cover to cover at least five times expecting a clue, a pointer, but got nothing.

Halfway through the tumultuous decade, exactly four months after a sudden divorce, on Thanksgiving night, sweet Ramana, the Maharshi, made a dramatic entry into my life. The vision was so real and packed with such power that my inner being reverberated with peace and calm for years. The greatest of gurus embraced me, walked with me arm in arm and lifted me up with infinite tenderness into his arms when I wept copious tears at his feet. His touch was heavenly, and I was completely bowled over. My savior assured me through more dreams that I was loved and under his protection. So far, he was the only one who drenched me with his unquestioning, unconditional love. All this happened without my even thinking about him consciously although I had read a little about him. Perhaps the system's innate intelligence senses what we need most at a given time and throws out the perfect solution.

I soon gave up japa and embarked on Ramana's path of self-enquiry convinced that this was it. However, as years went by, the enquiry was not at all addressing my innermost conflicts and the goal was still elusive. I began to wonder if the path was a dead end. There was an insurmountable wall in front of me that no amount of effort on my part was able to surmount. The 'I' was very much alive and my marvelous esoteric experiences did not change anything fundamentally. I remember Guha's words, "Those who come to you through books (like Ramana or Ramakrishna) and those who you meet face to face are two different things." Unfortunately, I could not bring myself to discuss my frustrations and doubts with my fellow practitioners. I was afraid they would chide me for lack of faith and devotion to Ramana. I was afraid they would try to convince me to persevere with my practices and one day Ramana would bestow his grace on me. I was getting desperate…

A few weeks later, a guardian angel came to my rescue and uttered the name of U.G. Krishnamurti in my ears. Had I heard of him? No, not really. Out of curiosity, I searched online and instantaneously found vast material dedicated to the fiery "non-guru". Tentatively, I started reading the *Mystique of Enlightenment* and it was like oh my god, finally someone was saying the way things were. I was astonished at his brazenly bold pronouncements which contradicted every belief I cherished. Till I read U.G. it never occurred to me that the whole gamut of spirituality was a big sham, a means to exploit the gullibility of people. For me, no more holy men, no more gods, no more enlightenment. The shop was closed, lock, stock and barrel. *Trust your own self and stand on your own two feet.* The point was driven home with *to be yourself requires extraordinary intelligence. You are blessed with that intelligence; nobody need give it to you; nobody can take it away from you. He who lets that express itself in its own way is a "Natural Man"*. I read the entire book in one sitting. I was hungry for more and could not stop until I had devoured every word U.G ever uttered. Later, Guha told me, "You have a tendency for fatal attraction otherwise why would you be interested in someone like U.G. and me?"

What a mystery this man called U.G. was. He was the ruthless Demolition Man and the Great Benefic at the same time. As the Demolition Man he smashed to smithereens all my prized spiritual experiences and lofty ideas about gurus, god, truth, reality, liberation, etc. All blown away in the U.G. maelstrom. They amounted to nothing, zero, of no value whatsoever and no way out of the status quo. As the Great Benefic, U.G. forced me to reevaluate and reanalyze my core, basic objective of liberation. He made me realize that it was a hollow and empty goal because it was purely conceptual. I had been chasing a rainbow. He made me understand that if there was anything called self-realization, there was nothing I could do to achieve it. Any movement, on any level would, in fact, strengthen that momentum. "Give up!" was U.G.'s mantra. Before long, I began to feel miraculously unencumbered, as if a heavy burden had been lifted from me. I must add here that to really imbibe U.G. philosophy one has to be brutally honest with themselves. Only then can the purge begin. Incidentally, Jupiter has been crowned the Great Benefic, the planet of luck and good fortune. Its beneficial energy is supposed to bring about transformation, radical or otherwise, in epic proportions. Bizarre as it may sound, my zodiac sign was going through a Jupiter transit during the time period when I found not only U.G. but Guha as well. As they say, good things come in twos!

To continue, in one of the U.G. books I came across Guha's name where it was mentioned that there was a radical change in his system's functioning after being in close contact with U.G. I learned that he also lived in New Jersey. I was excited that there was a possibility of finally coming face to face with a "live wire", a living, "self-realized" person for the first time in my life. I Googled his name for more information, found Golda's website and the rest, as they say, is history.

A couple of months after my first meeting with Guha, one fine day he decided to stop by for lunch at my house. The nimbus clouds dispersed, and it was as if I saw the sun shining for the first time in my life. All the pent-up grief and anguish bottled up for so long came gushing out as the emotional dam burst. For me, it was a kind of a rebirth, rejuvenation. Guha gave me the strength and courage to believe in myself. He made me aware that I was lovable, worthy, talented, and more than capable of living life on my own terms. He set me on a path to be free of devastating conditionings. From my own example and observations, whosoever has come to Guha has benefited in some way or another. Back to Nish.

Nish: Is the universe deterministic?

Guha: What will you do knowing that? If someone says yes, you want to have proof.

Nish is curious why U.G. wanted Guha to find and read an early Bengali edition of *The Gospel of Sri Ramakrishna*. Guha replies the context in which U.G. asked him to do so was not for any noble purpose but to find out whether Ramakrishna may have used profanity. U.G. had started using foul language and was looking to find justification in spiritual literature. English editions, including the one I had read years ago, do not contain any bad words, if at all they were used by RK. Guha ended up reading the book from cover to cover and marked sections which he thought may be pertinent for U.G's purpose. The talk continues. I am sitting next to Guha and it is becoming difficult for me to concentrate on what's being said. My eyelids are drooping and by sheer will I am trying not to doze off. I have seen this happen many times. On one occasion, I felt a kind of expansion in my consciousness when he was giving a lengthy talk.

Guha (later): You don't create life, you are just a medium. You don't know what's going on there, neither mother nor father. Out of knowledge you get confidence, but that fictitious confidence has a very limited and functional aspect.

Listening to him I am reminded of a talk he gave on how we seek to create artificial reality through knowledge:

Every intention comes out of the sublime desire to be alive. It's inbuilt in the species. Out of this, the intention of the knowledge is born. However, you want a secure future and to be free from the fear of the unknown by using knowledge and creating a virtual reality. The unknown can never be part of the knowledge and that's what the seeker is seeking.

Knowledge will never satisfy the knower and the fear of the unknown will never go. Your well-thought-out virtual reality will always break down as life unfolds and shatters your expectations. Understand, there can never be any knowledge which will give you complete security. All that your knowledge will create is an artificial security and that artificial security or reality can never take care of everything. It is betraying you every second. The moment you create an artificial reality you are micromanaging living moments and the moment an outcome is not as expected, it all comes crashing down. Life is moving in its own way, not through your picture-perfect reality. We have very little choice but to accept the power of life and its unknowability of movements towards the future. That's the only way it can be dealt the best. The desire for knowledge needs to come to an end. It's a meaningless search to know the unknown and control uncertainty.

~

Chapter Twelve

A True Friend

Freedom is when the oppressive nature of the sense of self somehow begins to peel off from a personality; then its effect is very different. It is not an idea of perfection. The brain is not going to alter but the nature of the drive is going to be very different. The individual can function in his own innate way.
– Guha

June 20, 2015
New Jersey

Dearest Guha: ... Your presence creates an atmosphere of transparency and freedom and unexpectedly – fun! What could be better? Hard to believe it's all real because the society that made me, taught me, "loved" me, etc., made it its business to blind me to reality. Still am blind. Will probably die blind. But a little snake of something or other is always sneaking around inside my body, a subversive untamed something that knows it is all shit. I thank you for encouraging my little snake. I'm lucky to have been in the right place at the right time. First I met U.G. Then I met you. Lucky Luna!

– Luna Tarlo in Introduction to *Guha Talks to the Mother of God*

Luna Tarlo, unknowingly perhaps, made a bombshell declaration in the excerpt above. If one carefully analyzes what Luna is proclaiming, they will be astounded to find an uncanny resemblance between her modern-day pronouncements and that of an age-old Vedic prayer. In the ancient invocation, the seeker is pleading for freedom from misunderstandings regarding himself, the universe and god, all the while yearning for true knowledge. Similarly, Luna laments that she has been deceived and blinded to reality (asat) by the society but feels grateful to U.G. and Guha for leading her to truth (sat) by opening her eyes to all the "shit". She also thanks Guha for encouraging that little snake in her to dance to the rhythm of freedom. This hankering after truth seems to be inbuilt in the human species and is expressed beautifully in a *sloka* from the Brihadaranyaka Upanishad: *Lead me from falsehood (ignorance) to truth, Lead me from darkness to light, Lead me from death to immortality, Om peace, peace, peace.* In Sanskrit it reads:

asato mā sad gamaya,
tamaso mā jyotir gamaya,
mṛtyor mā amṛtaṃ gamaya,
Om shanti~ shanti~ shanti hi~~

The passage got me curious to learn more about this remarkable woman's extraordinary life. Luna first met Guha in 1995 and intuitively knew that "he was the best thing that ever happened to me". Over time, as her love and friendship with him intensified, she admitted in Introduction to *Guha Talks*, "The years of conversations with Guha had, almost without my conscious knowledge, changed me. It was as though I had been invaded, slowly, very slowly by some kind of grand common sense without understanding most of what he'd said…. Every time I talked with him, I had the same feeling, something was making deeper sense; my view of things was changing. I told him he was affecting me…" More than two decades later, her love for Guha has not diminished one bit. "If you really find a friend like Guha, your life is made," she tells friends. When

I mentioned this to Guha, his response was, "Why does one crave to be with someone? It is because they discovered that they are resonating (with that person)."

Luna has been living by herself for decades but now her health is deteriorating rapidly, making it difficult for her to manage on her own. She is fortunate to have her elder son Josh and his wife Pat close by who are totally devoted to making her life as easy and comfortable as possible. Till recently, Luna took the subway by herself to meet friends, do her own groceries and even work out at the gym thrice a week. On top of that, she frequented the salon regularly and I have always seen her well-groomed with beautifully manicured hands, colorful toenails and immaculate hair-do. However, with sharp decline in her health her movements have become restricted and early dementia is feared; she is getting increasingly forgetful and fuzzy about things. In fact, ever since I was introduced to her, she can never remember my name although she does remember that I don't have a job. Guha and Julie would conjure up funny names like kandini, bandini, fandini, etc. that rhyme with Nandini to make her recall my name. Every time we are together, Guha would ask Luna, "Do you remember her name?" And invariably she would shake her head sheepishly. Once after driving Luna from city to 42 Guha joked, "Your name was like a mantra, we kept repeating it to Luna so that she would remember it!"

The other day, she had a terrible nightmare and when Guha and Julie decided to check in on her, I too accompanied them. Luna looked ashen when she opened the door but her face lit up when her eyes fell on Guha. She was still shaken from the frightful dream where she felt she was melting or fading away and thought she was dying but was completely helpless to do anything about it. Guha listened to her with utmost patience but kept it playful and light-hearted so as to put her at ease. Consoling her that she had lived 94 years independently on her own two feet, he said it was time to accept that the body was slowing down and get full-time help. Luna, who dislikes that idea, did not reject it this time and kept quiet. The scriptures say birth, growth, disease, decay and death form the circle of life and each stage is inevitable but to watch a dear one desperately struggling to make sense of what was happening to her is terrifying. As I have said earlier, thoughts of aging and dying which have been nagging me lately are tough to come to terms with.

Luna and Julie go back a long way having known each other for over 25 years. They met at one of Andrew Cohen's satsangs and have stuck together since. Incidentally, Andrew is Luna's younger son who is a well-known American neo-Advaita teacher. His guru was H D W Poonja who declared that Andrew was self-realized and gave him the mandate to start teaching. Initially, Luna, the doting mother willingly became Andrew's disciple and attended his retreats like any other faithful follower, even going to India. As time went by, she began to discern a few things about her darling - that he was evolving into a power-hungry, manipulative and tyrannical godman. Andrew did not spare the rod on his mother too, subjecting her to repeated humiliation in front of others. Getting more and more disillusioned by his despotic behavior, sparks of rebellion began to ignite in her. As for Julie, she was introduced to the god man by her then boyfriend although she disliked him and hated to be part of the sangha. Both stalwarts got their break in California in 1989 where they were attending a retreat.

By now they had read about U.G. and had enquired about his whereabouts. Finding that he was in the Golden State in Mill Valley which was not too far from them, they wasted no time in arriving at U.G. Krishnamurti's doorstep. He was a game changer for both, to say the least. He confirmed their worst fears about being a "spiritual slave" and gave them the push they needed to take the next step. For Julie, it was love at first sight and she never left U.G's side till the last. For Luna, U.G. was the catalyst she was looking for in her "awakening". They walked out on Andrew two days later. Luna's indomitable spirit would not allow her to remain servile anymore, even at the grim prospect of losing her son. The subsequent estrangement between mother and son must have been truly heartbreaking but they reconciled recently after almost a quarter century. Luna has narrated her ordeal with candor and courage in her critically-acclaimed and widely read book *Mother of God* (1997). It is a must read for all "seekers of truth".

Luna was introduced to Guha on the day he went to meet U.G. for the first time in Julie's apartment near Central Park in Manhattan. They became thick only years later when once she began asking Guha a lot of questions and was surprised to find that she was resonating with him. Over the years, Luna's sharp intellect and inexhaustible curiosity led her to engage Guha in innumerable thought-provoking discussions. They covered the whole gamut of human experience, from the invention of "god", the nature of conflict and sorrow, the role of religion and religious institutions in society, to what Guha had come into. Realizing that these were no ordinary talks, Julie started recording them and it is due to her efforts that today we have a lovely book titled *Guha Talks with the Mother of God.* "Luna was the first person to tell me that she felt something different talking to me back in 2003," says Guha.

I approached Golda, a close friend of Guha and Luna to throw some light on how Luna related to Guha. Golda reminisces, "Luna has the deepest love and respect for Guha and would never tire of telling me that he had something important to say. She felt he had it, had got it through U.G. and she wanted what he had. 'I want what you have, that's why I hang around you,' she would tell Guha. She said, 'When I sit next to him I feel like I'm drugged; I feel this heat coming in my body.' She loved his confidence, his conviction and the way he received things. He definitely shaped her life in many ways.

"Luna was instrumental in connecting me to Guha. I met Guha and Luna for the first time in Switzerland in 2003. After we left, Luna and I would call each other frequently and she would always talk about Guha. She gave me all his contact information – his work number, home number and email because she wanted me to connect with him. She believed in him so much, that he really had something to offer and she was very persistent. The first thing she did was make me write down a quote Guha had sent to her because it impacted her greatly. *Don't look to the future because you never know what it may bring. All you can deal with is what is in front of you.*"

N: Is it true that Luna had fallout with Guha for a brief time?

Golda: "Yes, Luna did have her moments. There's a little story behind it. Once Guha was passionately discussing something with Luna and her friend Oskar and in the heat of the moment he raised his voice at her. This she found insulting, especially in the presence of a friend whom she really liked. I was also present at the time and personally didn't find anything insulting in what Guha was saying or think much of it. He was just very animated and loud. Perhaps Luna hadn't seen that side of him before so maybe she took offense at what she believed made her look bad in front of Oskar. Months later, she told me, 'Look, Golda, it had nothing to do with me, he was yelling at *you* (laughs) because I had done nothing wrong.' It is interesting and funny how she tried to deal with it and justify it. Ironically, she fell out with Oskar and went back to Guha."

June 22, 2015

It is afternoon and I am driving Guha to his home after a heavy meal at a friend's. On a small winding road surrounded by fields, marshes and farmland owned by Rutgers University, I spot a little turtle covered with a thick brown shell. The critter is standing on the edge of the road, as if waiting to cross to the other side. I excitedly point out to Guha who is sitting beside me. He cries out, "Stop! This little fellow will be killed!" As I come to a screeching halt, he jumps out of the car in the middle of the road, picks up the little one and deposits him into the marsh out of harm's way. That was a swift, smooth and sound operation. Next, I see Canadian Mother Goose running in the field with her three little ones following her as if their life depended on it. I was enchanted looking at this charming scene. Guha remarks, "The mother is training the little ones how to survive in this world." Oh, sweet love! On we go. Now a teeny, weenie baby squirrel with pretty stripes is scurrying across the road. One of these days I may perforce crush one of these wily but adorable creatures; they have a knack of darting right in front of your car when you are least expecting. I must have slammed the brakes a million times to save them. We continue and just as I was about to make a turn, Guha shouts, "Watch out!" "What did I do," I ask him in a panic? "Oh, it's okay, you nearly ran over a chipmunk. But don't worry, I didn't hear any crunching sound so I think he was saved," he says with a twinkle in his eyes. What in the world is going on!

The turtle encounter reminds me of an awful day I'd rather forget. A few months ago while I was driving to the supermarket near home, I saw an orange colored baby turtle right in front of my car. He must have walked all the way from the water basin in the nearby woods. I slowed down in time and veered to the left to avoid trampling it. I had a good look at this lovely creature admiring its attractively patterned orange-colored shell. I procrastinated whether to stop and move it to safety or be on my way. I chose the latter thinking others would see it, like I did, and avoid hitting it. Alas, on my way back, I saw it crushed, in a pool of blood! I was horrified and almost felt sick to my stomach. Till today, I feel guilty about "killing" Mother Nature's child; if I had acted with alacrity like Guha, it would still be alive. Lesson learned: Never drag your feet over matters of life and death.

One last tale to warm your heart. When I was working at a digital marketing agency some time ago, I made it a point to go for a stroll in the nearby state park during lunch time. On a hot summer day when I reached there, I was delighted to observe the entire animal kingdom was making merry – the birds and the bees, the squirrels and the butterflies, the ducks and the swans and the toads and the turtles.

As I glanced at the cove to my right, I saw a line of turtles perched on a branch of a tree which was jutting very low over the waters – not one, not two, not three but thirteen of them in a row taking a siesta! It was gladdening to behold such a happy, loving, peaceful co-existence. Perhaps we can learn a thing or two from them. Suddenly, my foot hit something hard and when I looked down I saw a big brown tortoise staring straight at me. Thank goodness I didn't stomp him to death. I gave him a quizzical look and did a double take when he winked at me (or was that my imagination) as if trying to tell me you'd better get back to work, missy, or they'll fire you. A few days later, I was out of a job.

June 23, 2015
Manhattan

It is 8 am on a glorious, sunny morning and we are lounging in Kamal's classy hotel room in downtown – Kamal, Julie, Guha, Manoj and I. The huge floor-to-ceiling glass windows all around the room offer breathtaking views of the city. Beyond the glassy skyscrapers, like miniature models, I can see the BMW spanning the East River. The closest and the oldest from where we are is the iconic Brooklyn Bridge, next is the Manhattan Bridge and furthest away is the Williamsburg Bridge – BMW – all connecting Manhattan to different parts of Brooklyn. On my extreme right is Lady Liberty on the Hudson with her torch held high promising freedom and liberty to all. Incidentally, the newly-built 9/11 Memorial and One World Trade Center (the exact location where the original 6 WTC once stood) are just a hop, skip and jump from this hotel. Standing proud with its spire reaching the skies, One WTC, colloquially known as the Freedom Tower, at 104 floors is now the tallest edifice in the western hemisphere.
Guha: My chemistry teacher would always tell us little knowledge is a dangerous thing. And to prove his point he would narrate this

story to us: Once a boy learnt in school that nitric acid dissolves copper. That day when he returned home he found his little brother had swallowed a copper coin which was stuck in his throat. He immediately procured some nitric acid and poured it down his brother's throat! J Krishnamurti used to affirm there is no totality of knowledge; it is always fragmented.

June 25, 2015
At 42

At my request, Guha is reciting the first Sanskrit verse he learnt when he was in sixth grade:

मन्त्रे तीर्थे द्विजे दैवे दैवज्ञे भेषजे गुरौ
याद्दशी भावना यत्र सिद्दिर्भवतिताद्दशी
– समयोचितपद्यमालिका

Transliteration:
Mantre tIrthe dvije daive daivajne bheshaje gurou
Yaadrushee bhaavanaa yatra siddirbhavati taadrushee
– Samayochitapadyamaalikaa

English Translation:
Mantras, pilgrimages, the twice born (brahmanas), deities, seekers/knowers of God, doctors, teachers – their usefulness (to us) will be proportional to the faith we put in them.

Guha: Now I think these kinds of *slokas* have placebo value. I often used to experiment about their efficacy and would invariably fail.

4.52 pm
Take 10 from Guha:

- *Buddha understood that the problem of mankind had nothing to do with finding god but the problem was of suffering. That's why he went to the root of suffering – desires. He realized that every drive to get pleasure creates that which is going to give you sorrow.*
- *Want is infinite, need is limited. We have created a social structure where your need is not innate but created by the society which is governing your needs.*
- *Even if you are sitting in a cave and meditating, that what you are thinking (or experiencing) is handed down to you from society.*
- *Everybody wants to be the best. Every Tom, Dick or Harry wants to be the best in class. How is it possible? You have to understand the reality of your existence. Accordingly, you must curb your imagination. If you do, you begin to find a new harmony.*
- *You as you know yourself are not in touch with the life that is unfolding inside you. And you want to control outside, you think you have the power to do that! The one who is unable to control what is going on inside is pretending to control what is outside. Can you imagine how contradictory it is?*
- *If somebody is honestly trying to understand and cannot, accept that they don't need to understand.*
- *Beliefs are social conditioning.*
- *Life has tremendous power. If someone has a very fast response mechanism you say he has magical power.*
- *The power of negation is very important in breaking habitual things.*
- *Accepting a goal of life as reality is going to fail and make you miserable.*

July 2, 2015
At Julie's

It is 6 pm and Guha is talking to an old U.G. friend who is visiting from Washington DC. In the early seventies when he was a teen, this

middle-aged gent used to attend JK talks in Switzerland and that's where he heard about the other Krishnamurti. Soon he became a regular at U.G. camp too and his love for U.G. kept him coming till U.G.'s death in 2007. U.G. used to humorously call him the "double agent" as he originally came to the US from Russia and no one could figure out what exactly he did for a living. I find him quite interesting, easy-going and immensely inquisitive about philosophical and spiritual topics. He and Guha are having an animated discussion while Radhika, Manoj and I are listening attentively.
Guha:

- *If things begin to operate the way they are supposed to, then there's nothing to do.*
- *The game of life is enacting.*
- *There is no such thing as average person.*
- *The process of life is vast; I pick up two, three experiences and give it causality. Our ideas capture a very fragmented view of life. Our brain is so limited it cannot even capture a moment.*
- *It was a different kind of freedom U.G. was interested in, not behavioral. That was a secondary aspect for him.*
- *'U.G. really, really showed me that I'm very lucky that I came to him.' All such thoughts are detrimental. There is no appreciation -do you appreciate that the heart is beating?*

July 7, 2015

I have not been able to write for a few days now. There's no plausible reason but I always end up feeling guilty. Manoj left for India three days ago which was my birthday. Guha said that was my birthday present. We were on war path the last few days and I had completely stopped talking to him. It was after that massive fight we had at Julie's. It started with something inconsequential but rapidly degenerated into a slanging match with numerous exchanges of *shut up, no, you shut up, get lost* and so on. Finally, he yelled, "I can walk out of here this very moment and never come back!" Without wasting a moment I replied, "Go ahead, be my guest, what are you waiting for?" After that, tense silence. He remained where he was and Guha and Julie kept out of it.

A couple of days ago, at Guha's request Manoj was reading out loud U.G.'s 108 Money Maxims. These adages may sound perverse if you have a stereotypical, conditioned mindset. Ludicrous or not, when *Make others sweat. Enjoy the fruits thereof* was being read out, Guha looked at me and I would like to believe, "blessed" me with "tathaastu" (so be it).

Last evening, K and I were engaged in a heated argument via texts. It started when I sent him a sticker to wish him good night.
K: These bloody stickers have become utterly boring!
I: Everything in life is like that. You'll find me boring very soon.
K: (A volley of messages expressing outrage at such a thought) No! No! Omg!

The sticker ping pong continued till I again reiterated, "That's how it is, mind gets bored. Always seeks excitement."
K: But the body doesn't. It knows no boredom. In fact, it has a memory and wants to relive that without excess confusion due to multiplicity.
I: But that is just a concept for us, right? It's not operating that way.
K: They say mind over matter; U.G. said the reverse. Now you decide whether you want to listen to them or U.G./Guhaji. Have you seen people with multiple affairs... They are scatterbrained... Observe next time.

Talking about the mind and it's wont to seek excitement reminds me what Guha once said to me, "In the absence of pleasure the brain feels pain; that's how our brain interprets absence of pleasure."

July 23, 2015
Ansonia, NYC

Guha and I are waiting for Nish, Shujaat and Matthew while Julie just left for a dentist's appointment. Enjoying these precious moments with G, I try to get some answers from him.

I: How many people do you think are genuinely interested in what you're saying?

G: There are a lot of people who think they are genuinely interested but their interest is kind of a secondary effect. It is something they like or think of it as an alternative which can give them happiness, peace or solve the problems of life and things like that. I have found very few people who are genuinely expressing some demand, which is a very core demand of their personality. I have met very few people like that.

I: Which is a core demand with them?

G: Yeah, like genuine hunger.

I: For most of us that hunger is covered up by other...

G: The hunger was originally always there. It's a competition between your sense of expression as the life that is unfolding inside and the way you have been conditioned by the social system. So it is always a competition, a battle. Your system wants very, very, very genuine core freedom like it just doesn't want to be bothered. It's very physical; the system doesn't like anything that disturbs its rhythm, its balance, its functioning. Hot, cold, pressure, disease, falling particle, it has its own perfect proprioception of the material existence – what is inside, what is outside, how far it should be, etc. It wants to be free from everything that breaks down its order and poise and makes it unhealthy, uneasy or stressed. Similarly, the mental world – the world of information that uses the body – also wants to be in harmony in such a way that it optimizes the energy drain from the body. But the constant demand for continuity... the movement in the mental world is not a very acceptable thing for the system so organizationally it wants to free itself from this kind of stress, strain and wastage of energy.

We are on the 16th floor of this iconic building. (I always liked the name Ansonia; it has a nice ring to it.) Guha climbs all the way up here whenever he gets an opportunity which is a testimony to his robust health. Julie's apartment is a lovely, light-filled studio sitting pretty on one of the four round corner turrets. It has elegant moldings, a high ceiling and huge bay windows. If you step out on the balcony you will get sweeping views of the majestic clusters of skyscrapers framing the skyline, the ever busy Broadway, the historic Beacon Theater with is glittering lights right opposite and the 73rd subway station almost under your feet. If you are lucky, you may even get to see a falcon resting on the balcony railing although you have to be inside and remain quiet as a mouse. Julie once took a cool video of our handsome winged friend.

~

Chapter Thirteen

End of the Road

There could be a signal that can be felt by the system which is a lot more than trying to understand intellectually what I'm saying. Even the voice or tone can create a strange appeal inside you. This information can trigger some energy that is making a resonance to the other person. The meaning of the information can also trigger energy states inside. As U.G. used to say: "Attraction IS the action." The information by itself CAN trigger something. Information exchange is the first door for human beings.

– Guha

July 25, 2015
New Jersey

At sharp 1 pm I pulled up at 42 and saw Lakshmi waiting for me outside. We are heading to Julie's house for lunch where Guha and friends are already gathered. Lakshmi, dressed elegantly in a lovely turquoise sari with gold zari border, seemed relaxed and in a talkative mood. I was glad she was able to join us today since she is usually busy with a plethora of activities. Lakshmi holds a PhD in Physics from a premier engineering college in Mumbai and came to the US as a research scientist at Rutgers University. She worked till both her daughters were toddlers and quit for good only at U.G.'s behest. He would tell her, "Lakshmi garu, you will never be in want of money. There is an unlimited Swiss bank account just for you!" Now she is a dedicated homemaker, an avid gardener and a super cook who is always feeding an army of family and friends. In warm weather, she can be seen puttering around outside pruning her beloved rose bushes, lovingly tending the vegetable patch or just picking weeds. Her garden is covered in a riot of colors in summer and is the pride of her neighborhood. "Gardening is like therapy for me, my nirvana," she laughs.

Lakshmi is truly a remarkable woman given her helpful nature, readiness to embrace the vicissitudes of life and unshakable loyalty to her husband. Strong-willed and independent, she lives life on her own terms. Lakshmi shrugs at my compliments and credits U.G. with instilling strength and courage in her, "U.G. always said when someone has been around him all their potential comes out. In my case, my inner strength built up and made me fearless." Talking about U.G. her tone softens and she sighs, "I loved him dearly and will always love him. My relationship with U.G. was like that of a daughter towards her father. I felt like a beloved daughter who after marriage longs to go to her parents' house and just relax. That is how I used to feel when I went to Switzerland to meet U.G. every summer for ten years. He too treated me like his own daughter. We would laugh together, share jokes in Telugu and enjoy each other's company. Others would be amused looking at us and remark, 'you both look so cute when you are talking in Telugu.' However, I never had any question that I wanted to or needed to ask U.G. and I did not visit him with any expectations whatsoever. I never thought of him - or for that matter any of the other so-called 'holy men' I had met previously - as my guru. I am indifferent to such things."

Lakshmi continues, "U.G.'s message to me was clear - take care of your girls. He told me the same thing even on his deathbed in Vallecrosia, 'Lakshmi, go home. You have two very bright daughters, take care of them.' After U.G. passed away, I was going through some internal struggles and my mind was in conflict - should I make others happy or should I make myself happy? If I want to make others happy I have to make up stories but if I have to make myself happy then I don't need pretensions; I don't care. One day I had a vivid dream where U.G. sent me an email which said GIVE UP! In another dream he quoted a Telugu proverb *grahapatu, porapatu, alavatu* which roughly means once you start doing something by mistake and then repeatedly go on doing the same thing it becomes a part of you. I took that to mean I should be content and satisfied, no matter what the vagaries of life bring me and once that becomes a habit my turmoil will vanish. I followed his advice with all my heart and now I am calm and at peace with myself." We all have our demons to confront and I commend Lakshmi for being candid and painfully honest about how she deals with hers.

As soon as we walked in, Guha introduced us to Sam R., the new kid in town who drove an hour and a half to meet Guha. Perhaps he must have been taken by surprise to see such a big bunch, but here we are, all ten of us – Guha, Julie, Louis Brawley, Lakshmi, Radhika, Koushik, Nish, his wife Supriya, Shujaat and I. Sam has been reading and listening to U.G. for long but like many of us, never met him. He came across Guha material online and wrote to Golda and myself right away.

After lunch, Guha is ready for Sam. I am all ears, perched on my favorite spot - the U.G. bed. Incidentally, when I first took a nap on this bed months ago I saw a blue light like I used to during meditation. This is also the same bed from which Ellen Chrystal fell off one night and on which Mario, a staunch U.G. follower, breathed his last a couple of years ago. Mario was only in his forties when cancer took his life. I hear Sam tell Guha that he wants to be free from the sense of 'I' and has been practicing self-enquiry to that end. He is striving to find out the source of sorrow or the source of the sense of self, since both are same. He asserts that he is not looking for peace or enlightenment as described in the scriptures but acknowledges his inability to end suffering. He has reached a roadblock and is seeking some answers from Guha.

Guha laughs, "Then why don't you trust Ramana and do what he says? Why come here?" He patiently explains, "It is impossible to do a fresh enquiry because Ramana has already given you the answers... It is not freeing you from the conditioning because you have to use your intellect to do the enquiry and that intellect is singularly incapable of solving the problem of your sorrow that you're talking about. So the conflict remains. It cannot solve the riddle of 'me' as 'I' is *samskara,* it is the conditioning."

Guha continues:

- *Nobody can give anything to anybody. That's for sure. Mind is very tricky. By repeated thinking anything can become a reality.*
- *The power of the life force is working there to give you what you need.*
- *The demand from the sense of I is always in the known.*
- *Whom are you going to listen to, to address your equilibrium? You have to fight right where you are and find a solution for yourself.*
- *Social dynamics is a game, like you play a game of chess... If you don't want anything then nobody can touch you. Nobody can give you that magical power where no problem will exist and there will be peace ever after.*
- *Buddha said there is an end to suffering. Sorrow comes from expectations. Belief is the source of sorrow.*

I glance at Sam who is listening intently to Guha. Although polite and well-mannered I get the feeling he may not be back.

July 29, 2015

Guha has gone incommunicado since last two days and it is driving me insane! He has switched off his phone, so there's no way to communicate with him. Julie too has vanished. The only line open is the email which he is not replying to either. I have been keeping myself busy by transcribing Guha's talks, reading, writing, cleaning, cooking, walking, mall hopping, window shopping, and watching old music videos on YouTube - anything to keep busy. On the spur of the moment, I shoot an email to Guha:

Please come back to us!
Be with us!
Talk to us!
Walk with us!
Eat with us!
Have coffee with us!
Drive with us!
Take the long way home!
Don't ignore us!
Your silence is killing!
My hands are shaking!

Relenting, he texted a one-liner, *Relax, take it easy!* Although I didn't get to see him until four days later I was somewhat relieved and began humming to myself:

There are times when all the world's asleep,
The questions run too deep
For such a simple man.
Won't you please, please tell me what we've learned
I know it sounds absurd
But please tell me who I am.

Sept. 6, 2015

It's been rough on me these past few weeks. There are a couple of reasons for that. The first is when Guha told me he was not my friend – yet. Please note the "yet". We were taking a stroll in his neighborhood and in the thick of our discussion he got a call from

Kamal in Mumbai. As soon as he was done talking, he turned to me and declared Kamal was a real friend. I asked him wasn't I one too? *No, not yet.* A bit crestfallen, I could not understand why G would say such a thing. Here I was over the moon to have found a super friend like him, grateful to have him in my life and then this. After all, he himself has said many times that he never spent so much time with anyone as he did with me in the first few months. Tearfully, I recalled our previous conversation when I was casually mentioning some event in my life. As I was concluding with *oh but as you know, I'm all alone, I don't have anyone* he interrupted me with a*ap abhi akeli hai kya* (are you alone now)? I felt so loved and cared for then. Did I read too much into that? Am I not good enough to be his "real" friend? Do I need to prove myself in some way? With great difficulty I composed myself and we continued walking.

The second reason is more complex but like most other episodes with Guha this one also exposed my own emotional hang-ups. It had to do with the Guha website that I was building and was in a big hurry to launch. Towards that end, I was writing a short bio of Guha but before I could finish it he and Julie left for Switzerland. A little disappointed but undeterred I kept on at it and managed to complete it before they returned a month later. Impatient to get the site up and running, I managed to get a few minutes with Guha to get some clarifications. That same night, after making appropriate corrections and additions, the site went live. In my haste, I did not give enough importance to the fact that the photos were not that great. I thought I could always exchange them for better ones later, no big deal. Julie had promised to give me some but could not find them on time. To cut a long story short, I was bombarded from all sides next morning - the pictures were horrible, the headlines were faulty, some content was not accurate, yada, yada, yada ... Thinking that my efforts were being thwarted, I was sorely exasperated and unreasonably mad at Guha. In my heart I knew that he was simply pointing out what all needed to be corrected but I was inconsolable. No amount of logic or reasoning can douse anger; it has to cool by itself.

In the aftermath, our SMS' read like siblings quarreling:

I (early morning): You don't have any trust in my work. You keep asking other people's opinions.

Guha: I trust you! That's all that matters to me. I am not interested in (this) work that much. It's a problem of the sense of self. It takes long time to tackle such problems.

I: That's not true (about trust). Anyway, as you say it has to do with the sense of self. I don't want this damn website creating a rift with you. It would be better if someone else took over.

Guha: I have no problem, Nandini! You are my dear sister and friend, so don't worry about such trivial issues. You didn't come to me for work, so work is absolutely secondary for me. Don't let any issue come between you and me.

I (in a rant): You have to play an active role... the minute I ask you for corrections you show no interest, saying people in front of you are more important. But I say when you have a website or are working on a book you are reaching thousands. So you have to show more interest and be more proactive.

Guha: Wow!

My ego badly battered and bruised, I felt bitter tears burning down my cheeks. The mood was set for the rest of the day. I went to 42 in the afternoon but he did not broach what was uppermost in our (at least in my) minds. Guha was especially sweet and trying to appease me I think but I was determined never to work on that damn site again. I was ashamed to even look at it.

The following day I was still seething and resenting Guha for putting me through this, again wrongly so. Listlessly, I opened my laptop and started reading the monthly e-newsletter from Ramanasram to which I was a subscriber. Almost immediately my eyes fell upon a story about a devotee who was pleading with Ramana to give her updesa (instructions) since she was leaving soon and may never see him again. Ramana almost never gave spiritual instructions to anyone except to tell them to practice self-enquiry. He would say something like – ask yourself 'who am I' or find out who is it that wants updesa? Anyway, this time Ramana deviated from the norm and told the devotee to meditate on the prayer:

I adore Guha, the dweller in the Cave of the Heart, the son of the protector of the universe, the pure light of awareness beyond thought, the wielder of the weapon of jnana shakti and the remover of ignorance of blemishless devotees.

I was completely baffled, what did it mean? By the way, in Ramana lore, Ramana was supposedly an incarnation of Guha, younger son of Shiva. Guha goes by many names such as Kartikeya, Skanda, Kumara, Subramaniam and Murugan. I immediately sent a message to my Guha:

I: What do you say?

Guha: You are something, lady! People will die to get such a sign!! Should I tell the universe?

I: What is the sign?

Guha: Nothing. Only who looks for (one).

I: (Smiley face emoticon)

Guha: You are smiling, dear?

I: What else to do? I'm happy I got the "sign" even though it means nothing!

Guha: Now you are like a philosopher. Being is Nothingness.

I: All these words are like will o' the wisp; can't hold on to them to get something concrete. What am I looking for?

No answer. The word "shunyata" enters my head and I look up *Shunya Samhita* where it is described: *It has no shape, no color, it is invisible and without name. This Brahman is called Shunya Brahman. Atma Brahman is the space in the heart of the lotus out of which the phenomenal world is born.* It goes on to quote from the Mandukya Upanishad: *But since Brahman is unchanging, the changing world cannot be Brahman and thus must be unreal.*

Guha: Something unchanging is an assumption.

I: So we assume there's a substratum on which this changing universe is based?
Guha: The logic of unchanging is like your sense of "I", same from childhood until you die so they thought it was there before and it will be there after, so never born and will never die! It is just a spurious observation. Call (it) the witness principle. It's a faculty created by product of thought.
I: Brahman is just an idea? Isn't there a power which created, sustains and will destroy the world?
Guha: Yes, it's a model created to understand Nature. Is there anything in you that you can discover now that you think is untouched by any impression, thought, idea and image?
I: No. And I have no way of transcending them to find the "truth", if there's one.

Feeling light as a feather I am singing, *'I'm on top of the world...'* Very clichéd but at one time it was one of my favorite songs. After all, I am a victim of my conditioning, remember?
Guha: I am delighted for you, my dearest sissy!

I am even more delighted to be his sissy.

Oct. 10, 2015

It is Saturday and I have come to Julie's to meet Thomas the Greek. He is a young skipper who mainly operates pleasure boats and luxury catamarans in the Caribbean. When Thomas was here last time, I bugged him no end to employ me as his assistant-cum-cook on his boats because he said they make real good money. I was only joking, of course, as I can't swim to save my life and am willing to cook meat over my dead body. Nonetheless, spending a summer in the British Virgin Islands sounded very enticing. Guha would laugh his head off saying, "She is so desperate that she is even willing to work on a boat although she can't swim and is repulsed at even the thought of cooking meat." Not to appear rude, Thomas would politely reply, sure, if I took some cooking lessons, the job was mine.

When he was 26 years old, Thomas remembers being faced with life's existential questions after his grandmother just died. He recalls, "Stupid young me could not accept the idea that we are finite, and I got deep into reading books about longevity, so-called immortal beings and techniques to live forever." His interest in the supernatural, mysticism, religion and philosophy was awakened even earlier when he finished high school. "I can't say that I was actively searching or pursuing something, but I definitely tried to apply what I found appealing. I read a lot about philosophy, eastern and western, eastern being more fascinating and interesting. Finally, someone told me about U.G. and I started reading online and suddenly everything fell into place, everything that I had ever read made sense… not in a comforting, 'feel good' kind of way, but in a terrifying crystal clear way that I could not deny its truth. I had contracted the U.G. virus." However, not having the means to travel, he could never meet U.G. "When I found out about his death, I felt like I had missed the opportunity that comes once in a lifetime. Later on, faced again with the questions of life, I went back digging into the website, into everything he ever said, trying to find something that would 'do the trick' and relieve me from pain and depression. That's when I discovered the link to Guha's website and felt like I had been given a second chance."

Thomas met Guha for the first time in Switzerland in 2013. He says, since that meeting things have definitely changed in many aspects while many others have remained the same, "mainly me repeating the same mistakes". He continues, "What strikes me most about our conversations is the very personal and specific examples Guha mentions, it's like he sees through me but I never feel I am being judged. The one thing I notice is that after my interactions with him, I need to distance myself to see what unfolds, and to realize that whatever advice was given to me was precisely what was needed to be done. That advice requires strength to follow, which unfortunately I haven't always found. As I become conscious of that, I hope to avoid making the same mistakes again. What has also struck me is that no matter what the question is, Guha is always very clear with me, even with the boldest and most personal questions either for me or for him. No agenda, nothing hidden.

"As for the search, I never shopped around, I was never interested to see or compare. In a sense, I have been lucky in my life, whenever the need was there to learn, the right teacher came along. My search ended with U.G. and Guha. Nothing to look for out there; I just hope to have the strength to get to the end of the road."

Oct. 16, 2015

I finally found a job close by and since I am working full time now I have not been able to meet Guha much. Last evening, he was teasing me that I was too busy to spend time with him. I exclaimed that I was helpless, I was a bonded slave. His answer: *If you are really a slave of Mother Nature you are so powerful.* Whoa! That really got me thinking. This morning too I was mulling over it and texted him, "That's a powerful statement. Does it mean surrender?"

G: (Surrender) to what?

I: You tell me.

G: Everything that humankind invented, including god, has to go.

I: What does being a slave of Mother Nature really mean? Does it mean act from moment to moment without any desires, expectations, judgment of others, etc?

G: It's not something you understand and then apply to modify your actions.

I: No, it cannot come through the intellect. So then what does that statement really convey? Or is it something you keep in your subconscious?

G: You still want to understand, just putting it in a different way. Being aware is the only thing you can do. It all comes down to the intensity.

I: I see! Or do I? All I can say is there is this pain inside and the constant nagging to overcome it somehow.
G: Pain of uncertainty and lack of wish fulfillment.
I: Isn't that a lifelong phenomenon? If one desire is fulfilled then ten more crop up. And uncertainty and fear are also part of the psyche. Does vivek and vairagya help?
G: It's a practice so you will live in hope and die in hope.
I: Well, it alleviates the pain somewhat. Anyway, so there's no way out. BTSO (back to square one).
G: If it were successful in alleviating you wouldn't suffer in pain.
I: They make life somewhat easy to bear. Hey, don't take away that from me too! I'll surely die of misery then.
G: I'm not a painkiller, dear.
I: That I know. So you are implying better die than live like this. I agree. Where's the hemlock?
G: I can provide that.
I: Really? When? I'm ready to hang in the towel.
G: Point noted.
Another one:
I: Tell me, what is fundamental truth?
G: M O N E Y!!
I: I knew that was coming. :) That is a fundamental need to live according to social values. That is not Truth.
G: The one and only truth that human mind can perceive. There is no such thing as truth outside social existence.
I: You are saying money is the only truth we can perceive?
G: The word truth is an invention of culture Money is the truth of our fundamental existence.
I: Then what was Buddha talking about?
G: Buddhu, Dunderhead
I: No!
G: The problem we are facing cannot be ignored by the invention of truth; it doesn't work. Your CEO wouldn't be there otherwise to

unleash such an effect on others.

I: You keep addressing the problems of day to day living. I'm not interested in that. I want to know from you how do I find the Truth….the kind the Buddha, Ramana, U.G. enjoyed and now you. You all were not looking for money, were you? (After one hour)

I: Hey, you are not replying?

G: You are not serious.

I: What are you implying? Are you saying if I was serious something could happen?

G: I'm not saying anything!!

I: Hey, don't back track! Don't try to wriggle out. Tell me the truth.

G: If it were a bunch of words you wouldn't be asking me.

I: Of course not. I can get that from any book. I want what you have.

While texting with Guha I was simultaneously forwarding our messages to K.

I to K: Somehow I just can't swallow that there's nothing beyond money. What do you say?

K: The asker of the question is Nandini. For her money IS the most important thing to put her in a comfort zone. With the throb of life pulsing away incessantly only food is required to continue….shelter to ward off climatic extremes and predator attacks….clothing to cover and protect against weather phenomena… Hence, QED.

I: So should I not ask any fundamental questions? Should I stop seeking?

K: Money is the oxygen for Nandini.

I: Well, but she senses there's more to life than money. What should she do? The money will come hook or by crook anyway.

K: What more (do you need) than food, shelter, clothing? Procreation being one of the biological functions has been carried out…so your contribution towards the species is made. Now just for your survival money is a must.

I: I am trying to find out esoteric meaning of life like the Buddha, Ramana did.

K: They are both external to you. How do you know that there is a meaning (to life)? There may not be any meaning attributed by the spiritual lineage and the holy culture.
I: Exactly. I agree. But that has to be MY discovery. What you are saying is also hearsay, isn't it?
K: Then continue till you discover. I say it because you need money; that's not hearsay, it is tangible. The body falling in its rhythm is an observation in U.G., G and few such people. That is not hearsay. I feel it all the way deep down in the body.
I: Your observations about U.G., G are still hearsay aren't they even though you may feel deeply. It is not YOUR discovery. And yes, money is a tangible need in the social context. No denying that.
K: Deep down I have always felt the falsity of this stupid culture. Let me tell you, it is internally driven. By reading you become a learned ignorant. You are as natural as Ramana, Buddha or U.G.

If you are really a slave of Mother Nature you are so powerful keeps churning in my head even when I am half asleep. I tell G merely thinking about it kind of makes me feel good although there's no way one can apply it in any way. What did K think? His reply, "Yes, (surrender must be) total, complete and forever because Nature is powerful." But Guha categorically says that it is not something you understand and then apply to modify your actions.
Guha: You still want to meet me, my once upon a time dearest friend? I never spent that many hours with anybody within a couple of months of knowing. Once I said to him, "Don't ditch me!" Swift came his reply, "I never do such things. People go away when they find that what they thought is not available through me!"

~

Chapter Fourteen

Who Are You, Guha?

I am just an ordinary, simple, average, biological being. There is no other being there. All along we have an image about ourselves. I sincerely worked to find what is that but found nothing. In other words, all I have is an image, nothing else. Other than that, it is just beats and pulse of life. Basically, we are programmed human beings and a lot of our programs take very specific turns due to our upbringing and social conditioning.

– Guha

Nov. 21, 2015
Manhattan

Guha returned from India just a couple of days ago and Julie, Radhika, Luna, Shujaat and I are at Ansonia for a welcome celebration.

Guha: Something happened to me that makes me see things differently. I don't find somebody (in me) that has any authority to use this body. It just responds (to a given situation). I don't feel grief, frustration or misery. When someone says good things about me it has no meaning for me. I don't feel bad if somebody criticizes me either. For example, many believe I could have achieved much more (in life) but I am not affected. Factual memory is very much there, like an elephant's….

There is nobody (in me) that is doing anything. I only feel physical pain or discomfort. Things come to my head when there's nobody around and I (respond by) picking up the phone to make a call to someone. There is no drive. I have no agenda. I think that's a great way of living. It gives me a sense of freedom that I didn't have before. I can't use another human being for myself.

Listening to Guha I feel as if my dying system is being pumped with oxygen. The room is so charged up that I am feeling high. Going off track he adds:

If someone wants to discuss something with me, they already have preconceived notions and they are seeking verification from me. If they don't get verification from me, they'll go somewhere else and ask the same questions.

Nov. 28, 2015

The other day I was browsing through Kishor's photo album when I spotted a side profile shot of Guha that set my heart thumping. I could not take my eyes off it. It evoked sentiments similar to those I had about one of Ramana's portraits - the stunning "Welling bust" by a Goan photographer by that name. In my opinion, the sage's ethereal, other-worldly expression puts Mona Lisa to shame. I quickly put up Kishor's pièce de résistance on the Home Page of Guha website and ogled at it in awe. Mysterious, unfathomable, bewitching – who are you, Guha?

Full of excitement I reached for my phone, "Guha, I'm falling in love with you…and your photo….if I had seen this picture earlier I would not have looked at anyone else!"

G: You must have some connection….dear! Thank god you did not see that picture before…

I: Really, you look like a distinguished philosopher, just my type.

G: Good for you, (that) I just look like…Imagine the reality otherwise…

I: Actually, you cannot be compared to a mere philosopher; it is just a manner of speaking. Every time I look at that portrait it takes my breath away.

G: It is a good sign, dear… something must be brewing up… in you!

I am so lucky to have Guha in my life. He allows you to fool around with him like one would with a close buddy. Besides, he has a great sense of humor and we have so much fun together laughing about silly, inconsequential things. As Luna said if you have Guha in your life, your life is made. Thank you, Guha, for you being you.

Later, I asked him, "What is Reality?" Guha: "It is also a manner of speaking. I look like a philosopher but in reality I'm not, so you can't love me… that is the logical conclusion. If I were a philosopher in reality you would have been in love with me head over heels and go gaga and go crazy and so on and so forth… Just having some light conversation with you, dear."

Changing the subject I informed Guha about my Ramana friend whom I had not seen in months suddenly appear at my doorstep this morning. He lives nearby and I got acquainted with him when I started a satsang group for Ramana devotees some years ago. An ardent follower of Bhagwan, he was piqued, curious, I don't know, but straightway came to the point - why had I stopped attending satsangs? Had I lost interest in Ramana, was I bored? Taking a deep breath, I responded firmly that I had no more inclination to attend any spiritual gatherings nor was I able to practice self-enquiry. Something in my system fiercely resists any movement in that direction. Incidentally, I handed over charge of this group to another devotee a few months after I met Guha.

Guha: I hope he understands the meaning of enquiry - to enquire you have to be free from prejudice and pre-existing ideas. If you already know the answer to the question 'Who am I', namely the witness, then that's not your enquiry.

I: But knowing is not being, right? It is mental.

G: There is nothing other than knowing… You as you know yourself are nothing but knowledge.

I: But I do have a concept of "other than knowing". How to get rid of that?

G: You can't! It is not your volition that can do anything.

I: Yes, I see but do I really? All these talks always lead to a dead end. BTSO!

G: Does it?

I: Doesn't it? I am still where I am. Nothing has changed.

G: That means it didn't take you to a dead end. Dead end doesn't imply a depressed state of bleak future. You are hoping for a sweet ending, dear!

I: No, I see dead end as no way for me to get what you have.

G: Not knowing is not allowing you to that rosy end. So you are unhappy.

I: Not unhappy but hankering after something which I'm helpless to achieve.

G: I don't have anything you don't have, my dear friend! You don't trust me.

Jan. 6, 2016

As I said earlier, ever since I started working, my rendezvous with Guha have reduced sharply. Although I resent that, I have come to terms with my functional reality that I need money, money, money! On the plus side, I do get to spend quality time with Guha on weekends and at least one evening during the week when he drives to Princeton to meet me. His solicitude spares me the 25-mile drive to his house in heavy evening traffic. We usually start with lively discussions over hot beverages and pastries in Small World Café followed by a leisurely stroll around town or inside the campus of Princeton University, weather permitting. This elite learning institution became world famous because Albert Einstein taught here from the 1930s till he died in 1955. Guha would tell us that we were walking in the center of the universe because according to him, two Princeton scientists while creating a map of the universe put Princeton at the center. In the hallowed precincts we sometimes walk to the art museum, visit the historic chapel or sit on a bench in the immaculate Prospect Garden. With magnificent Gothic-style stone structures and humungous trees with branches spread out gracefully shading the paths, the 500+ acre campus is a welcome retreat for us.

Talking of Princeton, a few days ago we were in the coffee shop nursing our espressos and lattes when I narrated to Guha the dream I had the previous night. A very aged Ramana, looking nothing like his photos, was walking on a platform in a big hall where hundreds of people had gathered. With him was an old woman with white hair who I presumed was his care giver. There were other people following him but I did not recognize anyone. He suddenly started singing in a language unknown to me and lifted his hands to indicate that the audience should also chime in. The crowd got energized and they all started singing loudly in unison.

In the next frame, Ramana was sitting on the banks of a water body with someone whom I did not recognize. In fact, even here he looked unfamiliar but I knew it was him. His skin was very dark and his torso was bare. I gently ran my hand over his back, from shoulder to shoulders saying, "Finally, I get to touch you."

Lastly, Ramana and I were sitting facing each other in a vehicle. Interestingly, Guha was also present this time, sitting beside me. In fact, in the previous frames too I felt Guha's presence but it was sort of undercover. None of us talked but I kept gazing intently at Ramana. After some time, I was overcome with emotions and began to sob uncontrollably. He kept looking at me steadily, observing me without any expression on his face. Finally, after some time, he took my hand in his and covered it with his other hand. When I looked up and glanced at him watery-eyed, I saw tears were rolling down his cheeks too.

Guha laughed when I finished and joked he (Guha) was taking me for a ride! Incidentally, in *108 Names in Praise of Ramana,* composed by the seer's most scholarly and life-long devotees Vishwanath Swami, his hundredth name is Guha - *Om Guhai Namah*. Who are you, Guha? Unknowingly, was I playing with fire? Like when I was a little girl I almost got burnt alive sitting in front of a small diya or a ghee lamp, like a candle. To light the diya in front of an altar is a ritual in Hindu households. The innocent child that I was, I covered the burning diya with the frock I was wearing thinking it would look so pretty. The garment instantly caught fire and the flames reached my face in seconds but luckily, my mother, who was close by, ran and doused the blaze with her bare hands. Otherwise, I would have been charred to death or scarred for life. In Guha's presence though the only things consigned to the flames are old, destructive patterns and unwanted dross. And you emerge from the ashes as a brand new person. A word of caution: if you try to impose yourself or be hypocritical or two-faced, then be prepared to face the brunt his fire and fury.

I turned to Julie, our in-house dream analyzer as her insights are almost always on the mark. I confessed to her that Ramana was my spiritual savior at one time and had nurtured me in a way no human had but those kinds of beliefs were gone. I found it surprising that he was still ensconced in my sub-conscious. She listened closely and concluded that his continued presence in my psyche was likely due to the fact that he had touched my "soul" at a very deep level when I was down and out. However, she added, it was also significant that Guha was present throughout the dream and was sitting right by me in the last sequence. I must pay attention to that fact.

While at work I try my best to keep Guha engaged by texting him several times a day. Otherwise it is out of sight, out of mind for him. Whether it's a punch line, a parting shot or a simple hi, hello, howdy do, whatever he throws back at me adds a zing to my day.

I: Hello and good morning. Namaste.

G: Namaste. How are you, dear?
I: Just another day for me; kind of bluesy but c'est la vie. Hope to see you.
G: Why are you bluesy, dear?
I: I don't know. It's been like this off and on for the last few days. Maybe it's my default setting or may be too much on my head. You tell me.
G: You are hurt by your family big time.
OR
I: Hi, namaste. How're you? What idiotic work one has to do to survive!
G: M O N E Y!
I: Isn't there another way?
G: The way is unimportant
I: Continue the drudgery?
G: NO WAY OUT!
I: You killed me!
G: I'm not delusional!!!
I: No, but how about pulling your friends out of such slavery?
G: You really don't want to!
OR
I: Namaste Guhaji, Happy Monday!
G: Ha, ha, ha! What's the difference between night and day to a blind man?
Topic closed.

Feb. 20, 2016
New Jersey

Last Sunday, we celebrated Radhika's birthday with a grand lunch at Julies' followed by a delicious dessert of raspberry mousse cake which Julie brought all the way from her favorite bakery, Maison Kayser near Ansonia. Radhika's husband, daughter, Julie, Guha,

Lakshmi, Shujaat, Luna and I happily crooned Happy Birthday to our friend as well as to Shujaat since we were unable to fete him in January. Just as we finished, out of the blue Shujaat burst into a song:

Guru aagya mein niss din rahiye
Jo guru chaahe so hi so hi kariye
Be under the guru's command every day
Act only according to the guru's wishes

Guha hardly spoke and seemed preoccupied reading and answering his text messages. Party over, we all crowded into Julie's car to drive Luna back to the city.

March 1, 2016

Guha is leaving for India soon even though it's been less than three months since his return. I called K from office hoping he would cheer me up but it was not my lucky day and the exact opposite happened. I inadvertently transgressed our unwritten code and in return got a sharp rejoinder. That was enough for the floodgates to burst open. I ran to the restroom to compose myself before anyone could see me. Mercifully, there was no embarrassing incident till I left office. Back home, I spent the evening listlessly with periodic bursts of tears and self-recriminations. With a laundry list of reasons why it was a bad idea to be in a relationship I gave myself stern advice: For someone who wants "to be free" a relationship is the last thing you want. Again Guha's words rang in my ears: *All relationships are fraught with pain and only a passing pleasure! Your dependence on someone else to make you happy is the very cause of your sorrow. It should have sunk into you by now that there is always this expectation to get happiness from your partner and the pain comes when your expectations are not met. What do you really want? Haven't I said it before that there can be no relationship with another?* With my heart pounding and head spinning I threw myself on bed. The room started whirling and I was sucked into a maelstrom of destructive emotions. How much time elapsed I have no idea but utterly exhausted and drained I zoned out. I woke up with a throbbing headache in the middle of the night and found myself reading JK's commentary on "Suffering":

How quickly love turns to hate, to jealousy, to sorrow! How deeply we are lost in the smoke, and how distant is that which was so close... We are now aware that we are lonely, without a companion, without the smile and the familiar sharp word; we are aware of ourselves now, and not only of the other. The other was everything, and we nothing; now the other is not, and we are that which is. The other is a dream, and the reality is what we are. Was the other ever real, or a dream of our own creation, clothed with the beauty of our own joy which soon fades?

Aug. 8, 2016
New Jersey

Last weekend Ellen Chrystal, a long time U.G. friend and editor of *Courage to Stand Alone*, was visiting Julie. Ellen is a gifted Tarot card reader whose readings are highly intuitive although she countered, "I do not consider myself a gifted reader but U.G. brought that out in me and so do Guha and Julie at times." Ever since she came under U.G.'s ambit she has been reading fortunes of friends. In fact, U.G. who took undue interest in palmistry, astrology et al, would never fail to get his readings done from Ellen. What kind of questions U.G. could possibly have, I asked Ellen. With a smile she replied, "He would ask the same questions every time, 'When will I stop traveling? What about money?'" Interestingly, she is using the same Tarot deck which U.G. had handled umpteen times with his own hands.

After a delicious cous cous and salad lunch made by Julie, Guha fired the first question, "Will I go to India soon?" I forget which card came up but Ellen said it showed different processes going on... could be conflicts (holding him back), different mental states affecting the situation and so on. She meant as if to say there was no clear cut answer to that question. I have heard Guha ask the same question to her on an earlier occasion also and that time too the answer was similar. This is because he is always experiencing fierce push and pull from his friends. Whether in India, US or elsewhere, everyone wants to have exclusive time with him and the minute he starts talking about going someplace he has to face tremendous resistance from friends. If he's in India, his friends want him to stay there forever while those of us in U.S. constantly bombard him with texts, calls and video chats entreating him to return pronto. I have been witnessing this tug of war ever since I've known Guha. What a game!

Guha's next question was, "Will I go to Detroit soon?" Revathi who lives in Detroit leaves no stone unturned to be with Guha and perhaps Guha senses that intensity in her and tries his best to meet her as often as he can. This time the card he pulled was the Three of Swords. The imagery on the card is so ominous with its red, bleeding heart with three swords piercing its center that just looking at it gave me the goose bumps. But the intriguing part is though the swords are entrenched deep, the heart is still shown intact, not shattered like broken glass as one would expect. Ellen said it signified intense trying times, adding it had nothing to do with the conventional meaning of betrayal in a love relationship or anything like that. Later, I did some research and found that the card speaks of difficult times. One interpretation reads: *Three of Swords speaks of loss and difficulty, of sacrifice and broken relationships.* I wonder what such a card represents for someone like Guha who has no "emotional attachments" in the traditional sense. I heard him murmur, "It has come to this now."

Now it was my turn. I pulled the first card without asking any question to Ellen and came up with Seven of Pentacles. Ellen said it indicated wealth, style, elegance and that I will do things in comfort, that I liked my comforts. I asked her if I would be able to travel. Ellen said I already had the money or wealth, so yes. Guha quipped, "But money is the only thing she is worried about!"

Before I could draw the next card, I heard Guha, with a twinkle in his eye, whisper almost inaudibly to Ellen what about her love life? I pretended not to hear and cut the deck. This time I drew The Hermit. The card depicts a hermit in white robes with a flowing white beard holding a lantern with a golden star in the middle in his right hand and a staff in his left. He is standing on a snow-covered mountain peak, his eyes shut as if in meditation and the lantern in his hand shedding brilliant light on all creation. In my imagination, I visualize the Hermit's long, arduous journey into the deep, dark abyss of our consciousness with the light of knowledge as his guide and the staff of wisdom as his support to reach the center. Does he finally find the *hridayam* (spiritual center or heart)? Is that what the Universe was prodding me to discover for myself and by myself? I would love to believe all this but Guha's words bring me back to the ground with a resounding thud - there is no love, no truth, no enlightenment.

Ellen said I had drawn a very spiritual card and that The Hermit was one of her favorites. She said it showed a different, earthy side of me, a clear contrast to the material aspect that the previous card referred to. She pointed to the need to go into solitude, for inner reflection to find my own space, my center. This is now my favorite card too. I'm sure the wise Hermit will help me understand myself and enable me to find what it is I am seeking.

Aug. 16, 2016

K and I were discussing the subject of death a few days ago. Hindu scriptures tell us nothing is born and nothing dies, that there is no birth and no death for us, that life merely changes form, that it is indestructible. K cited ancient texts which claim when the life force leaves the body physical death occurs. Many a time I have heard Guha say that there is no death to the system. What then makes the living, breathing body inert and lifeless? I frantically implore Guha to help me understand.

Guha: “Nothing (leaves the body). You just don’t breathe anymore. Can you find out what is there in you now that will not be there other than breathing… other than your thoughts, feelings and experiences? The body does not “die”. The body’s resources are redistributed back to Mother Nature, down to the molecular level.

I: Is it all poetic baloney when they say when the life force leaves it takes with it the subtle body and latches on to another body so it can reincarnate?

G: Can you find out now that you have a subtle body or not?

I: No, but the sages had supposedly transcended the mind when they said all that.

G: How do you believe any of it without verifying some things - they even told you what you should verify. Since I’m not a teacher don’t ask me what YOU should do.

I: What will happen to this sense of “I” when this body goes?

G: This sense of “I” was never there; it is just a sense so it will go when the body goes. It’s your desire fulfillment through knowledge which creates a knower which translates all sensations.”

I: What about the sense of “I” in you?

G: It’s very much there when the system has to use knowledge to function in this world.

I: Only when you need to interact, communicate with the world? What when you’re alone, by yourself? Your system knows 100 per cent that you’re not Guha?

G: Yes. It knows it doesn’t have anything.

I: What exactly do you mean by that?

G: Just the information about my possessions and the relationship – my knowledge about things - defines me. I didn’t find anything else as self there. My search ended with a negative result.

I: The knowledge was not wiped out when you came into the Natural State? For example, I read that after the Calamity, U.G. could not

identify anything for the first seven days and had to be told this was soup, cow, bells, etc.
G: It was all part of a process; he chose to explain that way. No one taught him Telugu there (in Switzerland). He didn't forget a thing.... on demand it was available.
I: If there's no Guha then there's no agenda. So whatever I see in you is my own reflection? My own conditionings, fears, desires, wants, etc.?
G: Pretty much like that; a more complex mechanism is running at the back as a latent operator, through your *samskaras*.
I: Why am I so afraid of death?
G: The will to live is the last thing that goes away in a real yogi.
I: But why so much fear?
G: That's true for most people. Not to bother about all these matters is more important. To be worried about your fears is a new problem that adds load on the system.
I: Okay, but you see old age, disease, suffering all around you and you start wondering about these things.
G: So this is all in your imagination! Besides birth and death there's no guarantee of anything else in life. Love, relationships, marriages, jobs, even the weather – all the stuff that life is made of is unpredictable and out of our control. My birth I was not aware of and when the black van arrives, I will not be aware of my own death either.

I hear him out but the fear keeps gnawing at me. Through centuries philosophers and mind experts have been postulating theories on existential death anxiety and thanatophobia (fear of death) which they say stems from the basic knowledge that human life must end. Although Guha has categorically told me that I will never witness my own death, perhaps its indeterminate nature, of never knowing when or how it will strike is causing me angst. A moment later, I am giggling reading a post on "A good, successful death". Much amused I am tempted to present the listed death wishes to Guha and appeal for help to end my life story on my own terms by:

- Dying pain free
- Feeling good and at peace emotionally
- Dying in a location where the conditions are ideal, as defined by the person
- Having a sense that life's purpose has been achieved
- Having the people you want around you at the time of death
- Being ready to say goodbye

Goodbye.

~

Parting Shot

~

There is no such thing as ultimate reality. Functional reality is the only reality. The human brain conjures up images and thoughts by looking and listening; each brain is uniquely organized and different from another. However, we are myopic when it comes to recognizing this uniqueness. We think we can logically explain to others the way we perceive and think what appears to us as reality but that can never happen because the logic is completely subjective and biased based on our conditioning. All our belief systems are based on conditioning and there is no rationality and objectivity in the human mind. For example, the system rejects pain and we feel the pain of others yet we continually inflict pain on ourselves and others. This is the height of irrationality.

– Sabyasachi Guha

~